SO YOU THINK YOU KNOW

the OLYMPICS

Test yourself in these brilliant quiz books by Clive Gifford:

So You Think You Know Test Cricket?
So You Think You Know The Da Vinci Code?
So You Think You Know The Simpsons?
So You Think You Know Doctor Who?
So You Think You Know Discworld?
So You Think You Know Lemony Snicket?
So You Think You Know Shakespeare?
So You Think You Know London?

SO YOU THINK YOU KNOW

the OLYMPICS

CLIVE GIFFORD

Hodder Children's Books

A division of Hachette Children's Books

A Catalogue record for this book is available from the British
Library.

ISBN: 978 1 444 90685 1

Printed and bound in Great Britain by
Bookmarque Ltd, Croydon, Surrey

The paper and board used in this paperback by Hodder
Children's Books are natural recyclable products made from
wood grown in sustainable forests. The manufacturing
processes conform to the environmental regulations of the
country of origin.

Hodder Children's Books
a division of Hachette Children's Books
338 Euston Road
London NW1 3BH
An Hachette UK company
www.hachette.co.uk

CONTENTS

About the author

Clive Gifford is an award-winning author of over 100 books including *The Kingfisher Book of the Olympics, Outstanding Olympics, Drugs in Sport* and *Inside Sport: The World Cup*. A keen sports fan, Clive has visited a number of Olympic venues and is the author of the entire *So You Think You Know* series of quiz books. He can be contacted at his website: www.clivegifford.co.uk

INTRODUCTION

So you think you know the Olympic Games, the world's biggest international sporting occasion? Reckon you know all about the different sports and events, the cities where the Games have taken place and the outstanding sportsmen and women who have graced the competition? Well – this is the book for you!

Contained in these pages are over 1,000 questions about the Olympics past and present, from the ancient Olympics thousands of years ago to the forthcoming Olympics in 2012 and 2016. Each quiz contains 50 questions with the answers at the back of the book. There are two more gentle quizzes at the start to ease you in and two tougher quizzes at the end to really challenge you. Award yourself Bronze, Silver or Gold medals for fun! In addition, there are quizzes on the Winter Olympics and the athletes that take part in the winter sports. We hope you enjoy testing your knowledge and finding out more about this extraordinary sporting and cultural event.

ON THE PODIUM

Can you answer enough correct questions to get
on the podium and win a medal? Without cheating,
mark your answers honestly and then check below
to see how you've done.

Score

0–15   Hard luck, but you've just missed
            out on a medal.

16–25   Well done, you've won yourself
            a bronze.

26–40   Good work – you've scooped up
            a silver.

40–50   Brilliant. You went for gold …
            and you got it!

EASY QUESTIONS

1. In which country did the ancient Olympics start?

2. Which one of the following martial arts is not a sport in the Olympics: judo, karate, taekwondo?

3. Were the first modern Olympics held in the 19th, 20th or 21st century?

4. Are the Summer Olympics (the main Olympic Games) held every two, four or eight years?

5. If you came third in the final of an Olympic event, what type of medal would you receive?

6. How long is an Olympic athletics track: 200m, 300m, 400m or 500m?

7. How many interlocking rings are in the logo on an Olympic flag?

8   Which Olympic sport will be held at Wembley Stadium during London 2012?

9   In which country was the 2008 Olympics held?

10 What is the name of the Olympic athletics event where competitors throw a long, pointed pole as far as they can?

11 In a rowing eight, does each rower pull one or two oars?

12 Does Usain Bolt compete in cycling, football, athletics or swimming events?

13 What is the name, beginning with the letter P, given to the multi-sports competition for elite athletes with a disability held shortly after the Olympics and in the same venues?

14 What is the name of the wide road that links Buckingham Palace to Trafalgar Square, where the marathon will start in the 2012 Games?

15 Sir Chris Hoy has won Olympic medals in which sport?

16 Which is the only swimming stroke where competitors start their races already in the water?

17 What is the name of the one Olympic sport played in a pool of water with a ball and goals?

18 Which one of the following sports is not in the Olympics: badminton, table tennis, squash or tennis?

19 Which one of the following sports is not in the London 2012 Olympics: rugby, football, handball or hockey?

20 True or false: a man with a wooden leg won six medals in gymnastics at the 1904 Olympics?

21 The Aquatic Centre at the London Olympics will host which events – canoeing, sailing or swimming?

22 Which pair of sisters won the 2008 women's doubles tennis gold medal?

23 How many different events were there at the first ancient Olympics – 1, 7, 13 or 22?

24 Do men or women take part in the athletics heptathlon?

25 Which large river flows through the middle of London?

26 Which Olympic sport is nicknamed 'ping pong' and features a ball weighing just 2.7 grams?

27 Fred Lorz cheated during the 1904 Olympic marathon by secretly getting a ride in a car for almost half the race: true or false?

28 What is the name, beginning with the letter P, given to the platform medal that winners stand on when receiving their Olympic medals?

29 In a modern pentathlon, how many events do competitors take part in?

30 Including 2012, how many times has London hosted the Olympic Games?

31 Which is the only full Olympic sport beginning with the letter D?

32 Were the 1992 Olympic Games held in Barcelona, Boston, Berlin or Beijing?

33 True or false: the organiser of the 2012 Olympics opening ceremony is Simon Cowell?

34 Does Michael Phelps compete in football, boxing, swimming or cycling?

35 Which one of the following American cities has not held an Olympics: St Louis, Los Angeles, New York, Atlanta?

36 In which year did tennis return to the Olympics: 1968, 1980 or 1988?

37 If you were watching the Dream Team, featuring Michael Jordan, Magic Johnson and Larry Bird, would you be watching basketball, football or a men's athletics relay?

38   What athletics event at the Olympics features competitors swinging a heavy steel ball on a chain round and round before releasing it?

39   How many gold medals did Mark Spitz win at the 1972 Olympics:1, 3, 5, or 7?

40   Who won the men's 100m and 200m sprint at the 2008 Olympics?

41   The first ever event at the ancient Olympics was javelin throwing: true or false?

42   Does the Olympic triathlon consist of men-only events, mixed events or separate events for men and women?

43   In Olympic gymnastics, who competes on the balance beam – male or female gymnasts?

44   How many players are there in a beach volleyball team?

45   If you were flagged as offside by the referee's assistant as you entered the penalty area, what Olympic sport would you be playing?

46 How many athletes take part in the 100m sprint final?

47 From which country is famous Olympic swimmer, Ian Thorpe?

48 In which sport would you find snatch and clean and jerk events?

49 How many events do athletes compete in as part of a heptathlon?

50 At London 2012 there will be competitors from around how many countries taking part: 50, 100, 150 or 200?

EASY QUIZ 2

1 How many runners in a team take part in an Olympic athletics relay race?

2 Was Carlos Tevez, Wayne Rooney or Lionel Messi the leading scorer at the 2004 Olympic football tournament?

3 Is the marathon race just over 42km, 32km or 22km long?

4 In which sport do you find rings, parallel bars and a vaulting table: gymnastics, three-day eventing or weightlifting?

5 In which Olympic sport do players use rackets to hit a shuttlecock?

6 Did men or women take part in Olympic softball competitions?

7 In which event do pairs or teams perform routines in a deep pool with underwater speakers playing music?

8 A field hockey team consists of how many players on the pitch at any one time?

9 One Paralympic athlete has won more than 40 medals: true or false?

10 Was Britain's first gold medal at the Beijing 2008 Olympics in swimming, rowing or cycling?

11 How many events do athletes compete in as part of a decathlon?

12 What is Usain Bolt's nickname?

13 Cycle races for tandems (bikes pedalled by two riders) were a feature of Olympics up to 1972: true or false?

14 Was Argentina, France or Spain the 2008 Olympic champion men's football team?

15 In which sport does Britain's Tom Daley compete?

16 In which event do runners race over a long course and finish the race with one lap inside the Olympic stadium?

17 Which European city has not hosted an Olympic Games: Brussels, Rome, Paris, Amsterdam?

18 Are sitting volleyball and boccia Olympic or Paralympic events?

19 Does Shanaze Reade compete in cycling, archery, football or athletics for Great Britain?

20 In which Olympic city would you find Westminster Abbey and Buckingham Palace?

21 Were the 2004 Olympics held in Athens, Sydney or Barcelona?

22 If you were watching a server making a double-fault and the score going to 15-30, what Olympic sport would you be watching?

23 Do male or female gymnasts compete on the parallel bars?

24 Were the first modern Olympics held in 1896, 1908 or 1912?

25 Did ancient Olympic athletes compete naked?

26 Which Olympic sport features two competitors throwing jabs, uppercuts and hooks in rounds of action?

27 Does Ben Ainslie compete in sailing, cycling, diving or athletics?

28 Is the London 2012 Olympic Park north or south of the River Thames?

29 At which Olympic Games was the aquatics centre known as the Water Cube and the athletics stadium, the Bird's Nest?

30 Do rowers in sculls competitions pull one or two oars?

31 Were the ancient Olympics held at Athens, Crete or Olympia?

32 Do male or female gymnasts compete on the pommel horse and high bar?

33 At which Olympics does women's boxing first appear?

34 Has the United States, Brazil or Russia won the most volleyball medals in total?

35 In which Olympic sport do competitors swim, cycle then run all in the same race?

36 Can you name two of the three swimming strokes, beginning with the letter B, used in Olympic competitions?

37 Were the 1996 Olympics held in Athens, Atlanta, Adelaide or Amsterdam?

38 Baron de Coubertin was the man most responsible for the launch of the modern Olympics. Was his first name: Pierre, Louis, Michel or Henri?

39 What is the name of the martial art, beginning with T, which sees two competitors score points by making strikes with their feet?

40 At which Olympic sport do Victoria Pendleton, Wendy Houvenaghel and Nicole Cooke compete for Great Britain?

41 Were the second Olympics to be hosted by London held in 1948, 1956 or 1964?

42 Does Jessica Ennis compete in the heptathlon, track cycling or hockey?

43 How many gold medals did Michael Phelps win at the 2008 Olympics?

44 In which Canadian city was the 2010 Winter Olympics held: Montreal, Toronto or Vancouver?

45 Where would you find starting platforms, lane ropes and a false start rope?

46 In which Olympic sport do competitors use sword-like implements to thrust and parry?

47 Did women's football first become an Olympic medal sport in 1972, 1988 or 1996?

48 Golf has never been an Olympic sport before: true or false?

49 Which Olympic sport features aces, smashes, lobs and drop shots?

50 Which famous Olympian carried the flag for the Great Britain team in the 2008 closing ceremony?

MEDIUM QUESTIONS

1. Did the ancient Greek Olympics first take place in 776 BCE, 210 BCE or 44 BCE?

2. Were the first modern Olympic Games held in Athens, London, Los Angeles or Paris?

3. What is the only Olympic sport to begin with the letter R?

4. The 2012 Paralympic road cycling events will be held on what famous motorsports racetrack?

5. Did Kelly Holmes, Tirunesh Dibaba or Christine Ohuruogu win both the 5,000m and 10,000m athletics races in 2008?

6. The first ancient Olympic race was called a stade. Was it approximately 50m, 120m or 190m long?

7. How many metres long is a high jump bar?

8 Were the 1908 Olympics held in Paris, Stockholm or London?

9 At the ancient Olympics, was the first ever event: weight throwing, javelin throwing or a running race?

10 Which South African city competed for the right to host the 2004 Olympics: Cape Town, Johannesburg or Pretoria?

11 What nationality was the man responsible for reviving the ancient Olympics in the 19th Century: French, American, Greek or British?

12 How many Olympic gold medals did Sir Steve Redgrave win?

13 In 1996 did Donovan Bailey, Asafa Powell, Linford Christie or Frankie Fredericks win the 100m sprint in a new world record time of 9.84 seconds?

14 How many pieces of apparatus do individual rhythmic gymnasts use in Olympic competition: 2, 3, 4 or 5?

15   In what year did Michael Jordan first play basketball for the United States at the Olympics: 1980, 1984 or 1988?

16   After the 2016 Olympics are held, which will be the only continent never to have hosted a Summer Olympics?

17   What word, beginning with the letter V, means the place where track cycling takes place?

18   Is the director of the 2012 Games opening ceremony Steven Spielberg, Danny Boyle or Stephen Fry?

19   In which ancient language is the Olympic motto written?

20   How many boxers per weight division can a country send to compete at the Olympics?

21   In Olympic boxing is bantamweight lighter or heavier than featherweight?

22   Will the 2012 Olympic village provide accommodation for 5,000, 7,500, 11,000 or 17,000 athletes and officials?

23 At which Olympics were women's athletics events first included?

24 Which country does Roger Federer represent when he plays tennis at the Olympics?

25 What is the maximum number of points you can score with a single shot in basketball?

26 Misha was the mascot at the 1980 Moscow Olympics; what sort of animal was he?

27 Which famous British rower accidentally left one of his Olympic gold medals in a taxi in 2001: Matthew Pinsent, Sir Steve Redgrave or James Cracknell?

28 How many times has a Summer Olympics been held in the United States?

29 Which team ball sport returns to the Olympics in 2016 for the first time in 92 years?

30 In which Olympics was women's weight-lifting included as a medal sport: 2000, 2004 or 2008?

31 Approximately how many meals per day did the 2004 Olympics kitchens serve up: 400,000, 800,000 or 1.2 million?

32 At the 2004 Olympics which Middle Eastern nation sensationally knocked out Portugal from the men's football competition?

33 Which field athletics event was the very first to be completed at the 1896 Olympics?

34 How long is the swimming race in a modern pentathlon?

35 What is the profession of Olympic medallist Tim Brabants?

36 In which Olympic sport do competitors wear body protectors called 'ch'ong', the Korean for blue and 'hong', the Korean for red?

37 What did British sailors Alan Warren and David Hunt burn when they failed to win a sailing medal at the 1976 Olympics?

38 Can you give any of the three words used in the Olympic motto?

39 What is the name of the boxing weight division for male boxers weighing more than 91kg?

40 What is the longest race in an athletics decathlon?

41 Which former Olympic sport involves batters, a pitcher and nine innings per side?

42 If you leapt off a springboard to place your hands on the table, which gymnastics event would you be taking part in?

43 Did Daley Thompson compete in boxing, the decathlon, cycling or hockey?

44 Before she became a full time athlete, was Kelly Holmes a sergeant in the British Army, an airline stewardess, a bus driver or a member of the Pussycat Dolls?

45 What was unusual about the left leg of George Eyser, who won three gold medals at the 1904 Olympics?

46 Did Al Oerter win four discus, javelin or hammer throw gold medals in a row between 1956 and 1968?

47 In which athletics event do men run ten metres longer than women?

48 Man Afraid Soap was a member of which country's lacrosse team at the 1904 Olympics?

49 Which African country's people were granted a day's holiday when its men's football team won gold at the 2000 Olympics?

50 Which British Olympic cyclist's name is an anagram of 'Choir Shy'?

MEDIUM QUIZ 2

1 Where were the 1972 Games held: Montreal, Munich or Moscow?

2 In 1904, which one of the following did Harry Hillman eat all the time before

winning the 400m and 400m hurdles events: dried figs, hard-boiled eggs, kippers or unripe apples?

3 Over how many rounds per bout did boxers compete at the 2008 Olympics?

4 Which nine-time Olympic gold medallist's name is an anagram of 'Races Will'?

5 In what Olympic sport might competitors wear a protective mask and wield a sabre?

6 Kosuke Kitajima of Japan won the 100m and 200m events at both the 2004 and 2008 Olympics, in which swimming stroke?

7 How many medals did Usain Bolt win at the 2008 Olympics?

8 Which one of the following has not been an event at a modern Olympic Games: croquet, lawn bowls, live pigeon shooting or the standing long jump?

9 On what underground line would visitors to London 2012 travel from Heathrow airport in to London?

10 At the 2008 Olympics was the winning throw in the men's javelin over 70, 80 or 90 metres?

11 Did the Olympic flame travel by aircraft for the first time in 1952, 1968 or 1988?

12 Which British city bid for the rights to host the 1992 Olympics but lost out to Barcelona?

13 At which Olympics did Gertrude Ederle win a gold medal in the 4x100m freestyle relay team, two years before she became the first woman to swim the English Channel?

14 Which sport, beginning with the letter F, has appeared at every Olympics?

15 Did Wilma Rudolph win three gold medals (100m, 200m and 4x100m relay) at the 1960, 1972 or 1988 Olympics?

16 Hollywood actress Geena Davis tried to qualify for the American Olympic team for the 2000 Games, in which sport?

17 In which sport do competitors dance and move whilst holding and manipulating a ball, ribbon, rope or other apparatus?

18 At which Olympics was sprinter Ben Johnson banned for taking drugs?

19 Aksana Miankova of Belarus won which athletics event at the 2008 Games with a throw of 76.34 metres?

20 How old was Rebecca Adlington when she won gold medals at the 2008 Olympics?

21 Constantina Diţă of Romania won the 2008 women's marathon. Was she the youngest, oldest or most frequent winner of the event?

22 Which Olympic Games were the first to feature an opening ceremony: 1896, 1908, 1932 or 1960?

23 At which Olympics was a flame left burning throughout for the first time?

24 Which of the Williams sisters did Chandra Rubin pair up with to win silver in the 2004 women's doubles tennis?

25   Paralympic champion swimmer Natalie du Toit also competed in the 2008 Olympics, in: water polo, 10km open water, 200m backstroke or 800m freestyle?

26   Misty May-Treanor and Kerri Lee Walsh-Jennings won gold medals in both 2004 and 2008, in which sport: women's badminton doubles, beach volleyball, table tennis doubles or synchronised diving?

27   How many swimmers take part in an Olympic synchronised swimming routine?

28   Milo of Kroton won five ancient Olympic titles in a row – in which sport?

29   Which men's football team won the bronze medal at the 2008 Olympics?

30   Which former England rugby union player and coach became the director of elite performance at the British Olympic Association in 2006?

31   Did handball first appear at the 1936, 1960, 1988 or 2004 Olympics?

32 Which girl, the youngest member of the GB Paralympic team at the 2008 Paralympics, won two swimming gold medals in the 100m and 400m?

33 True or false: Henry Pearce won the 1928 rowing event by such a distance that he stopped to let a line of ducks pass in front of his boat during the race?

34 The 1924 Olympics 100m sprint was won by British athlete Harold Abrahams. His story was immortalised in which 1981 Oscar-winning movie?

35 Did Kelly Holmes win two Olympic medals in the 400m, 800m, 1,500m or 3,000m steeplechase?

36 What name is given to the short, hollow tube exchanged between runners in an athletics relay?

37 At which Games did the host country's laws outlaw boxing so there was no Olympic boxing competition?

38 Paralympic five-a-side football is played by athletes with which disability: visually impaired, amputees or those in wheelchairs?

39 In how many Olympics was rope climbing a sport you could win medals for?

40 Who won the most medals at the 2000 Sydney Games: Ian Thorpe, Michael Phelps, Marion Jones or Chris Hoy?

41 How many different men's boxing gold medals were up for grabs at the 2008 Olympics?

42 At the 2004 Olympics, which men's football team won all of its games?

43 How many goals did the same team concede?

44 Does one judoka win a judo bout if he scores two, three, four or six wazi-ari scores?

45 How many times in a row is a volleyball player allowed to touch the ball?

46 In which London park will the cross-country part of the three-day eventing competition be held?

47 Did James DeGale's Olympic gold medal in 2008 come in the welterweight, middleweight, bantamweight or featherweight division?

48 In men's field athletics, which has been thrown the furthest at an Olympics: the hammer, the discus or the javelin?

49 In Olympic show jumping, there are different coloured flags either side of each jump. As the horse and rider jump, is the red flag on the rider's left or right?

50 Stanislas Wawrinka won the men's doubles tennis competition at the 2008 Olympics, but who was his partner?

1 One Olympics featured a long jump competition for horse and rider: true or false?

2 The 114m-tall sculpture in the London Olympic Park is called The Summit, The Orbit, Winning or Londinium?

3 Did the men's 2008 Olympic long jump champion win with a jump of 5.05m, 6.87m, 8.34m or 9.02m?

4 How many different weight divisions are there in Olympic women's taekwondo?

5 Which sport has the most competitors at an Olympics, with around 2,000 attending the London 2012 Games?

6 If you were using a hoop or ball whilst performing to music, would you be taking part in rhythmic gymnastics or artistic gymnastics?

7 How long is an Olympic swimming pool?

8 Which London Underground line used by visitors to London 2012 has the most stations: Piccadilly, Central or District?

9   Do Paralympic athletes with cerebral palsy play five-a-side, seven-a-side or eleven-a-side football at the Games?

10   What event was added to the gymnastics programme at the 2000 Olympics?

11   Which country has won the most water polo medals (six golds and three silvers): Germany, Russia, Spain or Hungary?

12   What Olympic symbol did Baron Pierre de Courbetin design in 1912?

13   How many gold medals did Chris Hoy win at the 2008 Olympics?

14   When did Dick Fosbury stun spectators with a new style of high jumping: 1968, 1980 or 1992?

15   When was the last time that shooting events didn't appear at the Olympics: 1928, 1948, 1968 or 1988?

16   Is the lowest point you can score in judo a koka, yuko or ippon?

17 Which country appeared at the 1996 Olympics but was banned from taking part in the 2000 Games?

18 In which American city was the 1904 Olympics held?

19 Was the rope in the 1896 Olympic rope climbing event 6m, 10m, 12m or 15m high?

20 Which gymnast was the first to score a perfect 10 out of 10 at the Olympics?

21 Who starred as Tarzan in a dozen Hollywood films after winning five Olympic gold medals in swimming?

22 Did Nastia Liukin, Beth Tweddle or Shawn Johnson win the women's all-around gymnastics gold medal at the 2008 Games?

23 Which one of the following footballers did not win an Olympic medal in 2008: Carlos Tevez, Lionel Messi, Peter Odemwingie or Ronaldinho?

24 How many British boxers managed to qualify for the 2004 Games: one, five, seven or eleven?

25 Britain's Sascha Kindred has won eleven medals at four Paralympic Games (1996-2008), but in which sport?

26 Which South American nation sensationally knocked out the USA men's basketball team in the 2004 Olympics?

27 Is an Olympic trampoline 5.05m, 7.05m or 9.05m long?

28 At the 2008 Olympics, Ben Ainslie won a gold medal in what type of boat: Laser, Yngling or Finn?

29 Viggo Jensen won a weightlifting gold medal at the 1896 Olympics but also a silver and bronze in which sport: shooting, archery or gymnastics?

30 Was a triple jump event for women added 20, 40, 60, 80 or 100 years after the men's event first appeared at the Olympics?

31 Can you name the three throwing events in the decathlon?

32 What Olympic sport was, until the 2012 Games, the only event ever to be held in Scotland?

33 Hubert Van Innis from Belgium has won six gold medals, more than any other competitor, in which sport: archery, handball, judo or wrestling?

34 How many kilometres is the longest racewalk for men at the Olympics?

35 Nicole Cooke won Britain's first gold medal of the 2008 Olympics – in which sport?

36 Mike Gebhardt had to untangle a bag of rubbish from his windsurfer but still won what type of medal at the 1992 Olympics?

37 Which sport will be the first to be played at the 2012 Olympics: swimming, athletics, football or boxing?

38 What is the minimum number of points a table tennis player must score to win a game?

39 What medal did Amir Khan win in boxing at the 2004 Olympics?

40 Which member of the British Royal Family competed at the 1976 Olympics?

41 Does a men's shot in the shot put competition weigh 3.36kg, 5.46kg or 7.26kg?

42 Izzy was the mascot for which Olympics: the 1996 Atlanta, the 1984 Los Angeles or the 1968 Mexico Olympics?

43 Did Vitaly Scherbo win three, four, five or six gold medals at the 1992 Olympics?

44 The first Olympic basketball final was held outdoors in the mud and rain and the winning team scored just 19 points. Who were they?

45 Was Britain's only fencing gold medal won in 1908, 1936, 1960 or 2004?

46 Which Caribbean island became the smallest nation (population 67,000) to win an Olympic sports medal when Clarence Hill won a boxing bronze in 1976?

47 How long is the break between rounds in Olympic boxing?

48 On what piece of apparatus did Lu Li win gold at the 1992 Olympics, recording the last perfect 10.00 score ever seen at the Olympics?

49 Basketball star Oscar Schmidt scored a record 55 points in a single game against Spain in 1988, but for which South American team did he play?

50 Did Steffi Graf, Martina Navratilova or Venus Williams win the 1988 Olympic women's tennis singles?

MEDIUM QUIZ 4

1 Do swimmers in freestyle swimming races use front crawl, butterfly or breaststroke?

2 Beginning with the letter C, which country's baseball team won the silver medal at the 2008 Games?

3 Were the 1952 Olympics held in Tokyo, Helsinki, Moscow or Berlin?

4 Is one of the modern pentathlon events: rifle shooting, boxing, fencing or archery?

5 What is the longest athletics race held solely on the track at an Olympic stadium?

6 Who made a stunning world record long jump of 8.90m at the Mexico Olympics?

7 How many athletes did Tuvalu send to the 2008 Olympics: 1, 7, 13 or 26?

8 Which inventor of an electric grill won a gold medal in boxing at the 1968 Olympics?

9 Which one of the following teams qualified for the Olympic football competition at the 2008 Games: Honduras, England or Portugal?

10 Which country became the first South American nation to win gold at the Olympic men's basketball in 2004?

11   Did table tennis first appear at the 1936, 1964, 1980 or 1988 Olympics?

12   In what athletics event do runners have to hurdle barriers and cross a water jump on the track?

13   How many different forms of wrestling are Olympic events?

14   No Olympic male high jumper has ever won the event twice: true or false?

15   Which one of the following London 2012 venues will be dismantled after the Games: the Velodrome, the Handball Arena or the Water Polo Arena?

16   Which county cricket club plays at Lord's, the venue for the archery competition at the 2012 Olympics?

17   Is the highest scoring point in judo called ippon, wazi-ari or yuko?

18   Did Edwin Moses win two gold medals in track cycling, Greco-Roman wrestling, the 400m hurdles or heavyweight boxing?

19 Which British cyclist raced Chris Hoy in the final of the 2008 men's cycling sprint, winning silver?

20 What athletics event did Cathy Freeman win at the Sydney 2000 Olympics, making her the host nation's heroine?

21 Visitors to the 2012 Olympics in London may visit a 135m tall ferris wheel which gives great views over London. What is it called?

22 Which African women's hockey team were last-minute replacements to the 1980 Olympics but went on to win the gold medal?

23 How many points are required for a beach volleyball team to win the first set of a match: 11, 14, 21 or 25?

24 Angel Matos was banned for life after attacking a referee in which sport at the Beijing Games?

25 In which sport did India win every gold medal between 1928 and 1954?

26 In athletics, how many barriers do female hurdlers have to clear when running the 100m hurdles?

27 Which one of the following was not an Olympic gold medal-winning decathlete: Daley Thompson, Brian Clay, Jurgen Hingsen or Erki Nool?

28 Elisabeta Lipă from Romania competed in which sport at six Olympic Games, winning a bronze, two silver and five gold medals?

29 Only four countries won table tennis medals at the 2008 Olympics. Can you name two of them?

30 Which European nation did the USA men's basketball team beat 118-107 in the final of the 2008 Games?

31 Was cricket an Olympic event at the 1900, 1908, 1920 or 1932 Olympics?

32 At the 2000 Olympics, did Amir Khan, Audley Harrison or Lennox Lewis become the first British Olympic boxing champion for 32 years?

33   In which event would you find
      competitors in the water performing
      eggbeaters and scull moves?

34   Which year did men's hockey make its
      debut as an Olympic sport at a Games
      held in London?

35   Over what distance are all Olympic rowing
      races held?

36   Stephanie Brown-Trafton was a surprise
      gold medallist in a 2008 field athletics
      event – which one?

37   The ancient Olympics were originally held
      to honour which Greek god: Achilles, Zeus
      or Jupiter?

38   In which country would you find the
      headquarters of the International Olympic
      Committee?

39   In which sport do competitors wear a
      white uniform called a dobok?

40   How old was Ben Ainslie when he won his
      first Olympic sailing medal?

41 Which Scandinavian team won the 2000 Olympic women's football gold medal, beating the USA in the final?

42 In Olympic swimming, can swimmers glide underwater for up to the first 8m, 15m, 25m or 40m of the race?

43 Which nation won six Olympic men's hockey tournaments in a row between 1928 and 1960?

44 Was Dayron Robles, the gold medallist in the 110m hurdles at the 2008 Games, from Jamaica, Portugal, Cuba or Brazil?

45 Did 6, 13 or 22 competitors in the 2008 women's marathon fail to complete the race?

46 Who won the 2004 Olympic men's tennis gold medal – Nicolas Massau, Roger Federer or Andrew Murray?

47 In women's basketball, which team has won silver at three Games in a row (2000-2008)?

48　For which Olympics did the Olympic torch travel by jumbo jet visiting every city which had previously hosted a summer Olympics?

49　Which Asian country won both the men's and women's trampoline gold medals at Beijing 2008?

50　In seventeen Olympic men's basketball finals, how many did not feature the United States?

MEDIUM QUIZ 5

1　Which country has more than 300 million amateur table tennis players?

2　In what artistic gymnastics event did Louis Smith win a bronze medal for Britain in 2008?

3　The 1932 Olympic Games in Los Angeles featured gold medals made of solid 18-carat gold: true or false?

4 The high speed train which serves the 2012 London Olympics park is named after which object used in athletics?

5 Amik was the mascot of the 1976 Montreal Olympics; what sort of animal was he?

6 Teofilo Stevenson won a gold medal in boxing at three Olympics in a row, but at what weight: middleweight, flyweight, welterweight or heavyweight?

7 In what Olympic sport can you only score goals when inside the shooting circle?

8 British equestrian competitor, Lorna Johnson, was the oldest ever female Olympian. When she competed at the 1972 Olympics, was she 56, 61, 64 or 70 years old?

9 Standing a giant 2.29m tall, in which sport did Yao Ming compete for China at the 2008 Olympics?

10 Three new athletics track events for women appeared at the 1972 Olympics. Can you name one of them?

11 Off the coast of which English county will the 2012 Olympic sailing events be held?

12 Rebecca Romero won a silver medal in rowing at the 2004 Olympics, but in which sport did she win a gold in 2008?

13 A top water polo swimmer may swim as much as: 1,000m, 3,000m or 5,000m during a single match?

14 How many track cycling events will there be for men and for women at the 2012 Olympics?

15 At the 1996 Games, which male long jumper won his fourth Olympic long jump gold medal?

16 Charlotte Dodd won five Wimbledon tennis singles championships, but in what sport did she win an Olympic gold medal in 1908?

17   How long does a handball match last: 30, 40, 50 or 60 minutes?

18   Do 35, 55, 75 or 95 triathletes start each Olympic competition?

19   Which Olympics featured a stadium costing around £40,000 to build, with a swimming pool inside the athletics track?

20   Paralympic wheelchair rugby is played by teams of four on what other sport's playing area?

21   From 1997 onwards, what was the minimum age for a gymnast to compete at an Olympics?

22   What sport would you be watching if you saw an umpire show a player a green card?

23   Were the first drugs tests carried out at the 1968, 1976 or 1984 Olympics?

24   Bicycle polo was a demonstration sport at the 1908 London Olympics. Were the winners Germany, Italy, Great Britain or Ireland?

25 Which British athlete won a gold medal in the 100m sprint at the 1992 Games?

26 How many teams take part in the Olympic team rhythmic gymnastics finals?

27 Roberto Cammarelle won a 2008 Olympic gold medal in: taekwondo, judo, boxing or shooting?

28 Which African team did Argentina play in the final of the men's football competition at the 2008 Games?

29 In the 50m rifle prone event at the 2008 Olympics, how many of Artur Ayvazian's 60 shots did not hit the bullseye and score maximum points?

30 In which Olympic event are a horse and rider marked by a panel of seven judges on the accuracy and smoothness of their movements?

31 Is the total playing time of a water polo game: 32 minutes, 40 minutes, 60 minutes or 80 minutes?

32 Was the 1908 gold-medal winning Gyrinus a motorboat, a horse or Greek marathon runner?

33 At which Olympics did Steve Redgrave win his fifth gold medal in rowing?

34 At the ancient Olympics, was a *dolichos* a long distance race, a chariot or the pit into which cheating competitors were thrown?

35 Sawao Kato won twelve medals in three Olympic Games (1968, 1972 and 1976) competing in what sport?

36 In what athletics event are the western roll and straddle two techniques for clearing the bar?

37 Which Hollywood film inspired Chris Hoy to take up cycling: *Chariots of Fire, E.T. the Extra-Terrestrial, Breaking Away* or *The Bicycle Thief?*

38 Hubert Raudaschl appeared in nine Olympic Games, but in which sport did he compete?

39 Was Aileen Riggin fourteen, sixteen or eighteen years old when she won gold in women's diving at the 1920 Olympics?

40 Which country won four of the first five Olympic water polo competitions?

41 Which Roman emperor cancelled the ancient Olympic Games in the 4th century: Nero, Theodosius I or Augustus?

42 David Fall took part in the 1924 diving competition, winning a silver medal: true or false?

43 At the 1972 Olympics, the US basketball team were so incensed with a decision that they did not collect their medals. What colour were the medals?

44 At the 1956 Olympics, eventual gold medallist Charles Vinci had to cut his hair off to make the weight at the weigh-in for which sport?

45 How many riders compete in an Olympic BMX cycling race?

46 Hungary's 1936 Olympics gold medal-winning water polo team included Oliver Halassy, who: was deaf, had one leg amputated or one hand amputated?

47 Which city was supposed to hold the 1944 Olympics which were cancelled due to World War II?

48 Which Olympics was the first to be held in the southern hemisphere?

49 During the 2004 Olympics, did the Olympic torch go on a journey lasting 4,000km, 16,000km, 41,000km or 78,000km?

50 At the 1932 Olympics, Jules Noel sipped champagne whilst competing in which athletics event?

1   At which Olympics did snowboard cross make its debut: 1992, 1998 or 2006?

2   British skeleton competitor Alex Coomber used to practice her starts at home on a tea tray: true or false?

3   Shania Twain, Arnold Schwarzenegger and Michael Bublé were celebrities who took part in the Olympic torch relay of which Games?

4   In what Winter Olympic sport do competitors aim 'stones' at a 'house' to score?

5   Which one Winter Olympic sport combines cross-country skiing with rifle shooting?

6   Were the 2006 Winter Olympics held in France, Canada, Italy or Norway?

7   What medal did Shelley Rudman win at the 2006 Winter Olympics?

8   Do competitors in the skeleton travel down the track head first or feet first?

9 Was the 1976 Games mascot, Schneemann, a polar bear, a penguin or a snowman?

10 In what sport is the game divided into three periods of twenty minutes with each period starting with a face-off?

11 Has Italian cross-country skier Stefania Belmondo won 5, 7, 10 or 13 Winter Olympic medals?

12 Were the 1948 Olympics held at St Moritz, Chamonix or Salt Lake City?

13 Did skier Antoin Miliordos fall once, three times or more than a dozen times during his men's slalom run at the 1952 Olympics?

14 Which sport, beginning with the letter M, sees skiers ride off bumps and ramps to perform spectacular moves in the air?

15 At the 2010 Games, which country broke the record for the most gold medals, winning fourteen?

16 In which country will the 2014 Winter Olympics be held?

17 Which of the following British Winter Olympians did not compete in the skeleton: Shelley Rudman, Alex Coomber or Chemmy Alcott?

18 Bjørn Daehlie won twelve Olympic medals in cross-country skiing. How many were gold?

19 Seiko Hashimoto has appeared at three Summer Olympics as a track cyclist and at four Winter Olympics in what sport?

20 Which one of the following sports did not appear at the very first Winter Olympics: curling, biathlon, luge or ice hockey?

21 At the 1956 Olympics, which country made their Winter Olympics debut and won the most medals of any nation?

22 At the 2010 Games, which nation won both the men's and women's ice hockey competitions?

23 Anton Sailor became the first person to win all three men's races in Alpine skiing at the 1956 Olympics; was he Swiss, Austrian, German or Belgian?

24 Sonja Heine became the youngest winner of an individual Winter Olympics event when she won what event at the age of fifteen?

25 What is the longest distance raced in speed skating at the Olympics: 1,000m, 3,000m or 10,000m?

26 At which Olympics did Torville and Dean win the gold medal for ice dancing?

27 Which two Winter Olympics were held only two years apart?

28 Which country won a gold and a silver in the two curling events at the 2010 Games: Great Britain, Canada, Germany or Poland?

29 At the 1964 Olympics, Lydia Skoblikova won how many gold medals in speed-skating events?

30 In what sport did British women win bronze in 2002 and silver in 2006?

31 Eddie Eagan is the only person to win gold medals in both Winter and Summer Olympics. He won gold with the US four-man bobsleigh in 1932 but in what Summer Olympic sport did he win in 1920?

32 Which country came third in the medal table above France, Sweden and Canada at the very first Winter Olympics?

33 Was Sonja Heine: Norwegian, American, Canadian or Swedish?

34 Which two countries were banned from taking part at the 1948 Winter Olympics because of their part in World War II?

35 In ice dancing, how many different performances does each pair of competitors make?

36 At which Summer Olympics did figure-skating events debut?

37 Was the 1960 Winter Olympics held in Innsbruck, Squaw Valley or Calgary?

38 Which figure skater's ex-husband organised an attack on rival skater Nancy Kerrigan so that she wouldn't compete in the 1994 Olympics?

39 Was the first Winter Paralympics held in 1976, 1988 or 2002?

40 What was the name of the snowboarder who celebrated prematurely during the 2006 snowboard cross final, fell, and lost the race to Tanja Frieden?

41 Which future American president opened the 1932 Winter Olympics at Lake Placid?

42 Skeleton first debuted at the 1928 Olympics. How many other Winter Olympics has it so far been a part of?

43 How many snowboarders qualify for the final of the half pipe competition?

44 How many medals did Great Britain win at the 2010 Winter Olympics: one, three, five or seven?

45 Claudia Pechstein won medals in five different Winter Olympics in which sport?

46 Which European country finished second in the 2010 Winter Olympics medal table with 30 medals in total?

47 Can you name either the Asian nation or the European nation that Russia beat to host the 2014 Winter Olympics?

48 In 2002, Steven Bradbury was coming last in the 1,000m speed-skating final when all three skaters ahead of him crashed, allowing him to cross the line first and win which country's first Winter Olympics gold medal?

49 Aleksandr Bortyuk had a mishap at the start of his four-man bobsleigh run at the 1992 Olympics. Did he: fall and not enter the bob, land on top of the bobsleigh or enter the bobsleigh facing backwards?

50 Brothers Philipp and Simon Schoch competed against each other in the two-person final of which 2006 event?

1 Which country does Rafael Nadal represent when he plays tennis at the Olympics?

2 Boxer Ali Kazemi was disqualified at the 1992 Olympics for forgetting what items?

3 What was the first Asian country to host the Olympics?

4 Did Beth Tweddle, Louis Smith or Hannah Whelan win Britain's first individual gymnastics medal since 1908?

5 Which leading swimming Olympic medallist's name is an anagram of 'Help Isle Champ'?

6 Name one of the three sports that George Eyser, a man with a wooden leg, won medals in at the 1904 Olympics?

7 Which country has won all the team and individual gold medals in rhythmic gymnastics since 2000?

8 In the Olympic motto, does the word 'altius' mean higher, more powerful or faster?

9 Which one of the following teams qualified for the Olympic football competition at the 2008 Games: Spain, Serbia or Sudan?

10 What is the longest race run as part of a women's heptathlon?

11 What was the last Olympics at which Great Britain led the medal table?

12 Did fourteen-year-old Tom Daley finish third, seventh, thirteenth or twenty-second in the 2008 Olympics men's 10m platform diving competition?

13 Which country won the most archery medals at the 2008 Olympics?

14 Harold Sakata won a silver medal at the 1948 Olympics but went on to become which famous James Bond film villain?

15 ... and in what sport did he win his silver medal?

16 How long in kilometres is the cycle ride in an Olympic triathlon competition?

17   In the final of the 2008 women's team sabre fencing competition, did the United States, Italy or the Ukraine beat China 45-44?

18   How old was Jennifer Capriati when she won the 1992 Olympic women's singles tennis competition?

19   Were the first cycling events for women held at the 1960, 1972, 1984 or 1992 Games?

20   What sort of animal was Waldi, the first named summer Olympic Games mascot who appeared in Munich in 1972?

21   At which Olympics did mountain biking make its debut as a medal sport?

22   At the Paralympics, are judo bouts held between athletes who are: amputees, in a wheelchair, suffering from cerebral palsy or visually impaired?

23   At which Olympics were lifesaving and ballooning demonstration sports?

24 Which two-time decathlon gold medallist snapped his pole during the pole vault at the 1988 Olympics?

25 How much does a men's discus weigh: 1kg, 2kg, 4kg or 8kg?

26 Freyja Prentice represents which country at the modern pentathlon?

27 Aleksandr Karelin won the 1996 Greco-Roman wrestling competition without conceding a single point: true or false?

28 Laszlo Papp was the first boxer to win a gold medal at three Olympics in a row. Was he from Hungary, Belgium, Poland or Denmark?

29 Did Steven Hooker, Sergey Bubka or Brad Walker win the 2008 men's pole vault competition with an Olympic record vault of 5.96m?

30 At the 1924 Olympics boxing competition, was Roger Brousse eventually disqualified for biting Henry Mallin's finger, ear, or chest?

31 In which cycling event was Julien Absalon the Olympic champion in both 2004 and 2008?

32 How many official mascots were there for the 2008 Olympics in Beijing?

33 Badminton first appeared as an Olympic medal sport at which Games?

34 In what Paralympic sport must competitors bounce or throw the ball after every two pushes of the wheels of their wheelchair?

35 At which Olympics did women's wrestling appear for the first time?

36 Is the Olympic record for the men's triple jump over 14m, over 15.5m, over 16.5m or over 18m?

37 The 2012 Olympic torch relay begins in May 2012 at which British location: Edinburgh Castle, Land's End, Buckingham Palace or Alton Towers?

38 Which British woman became the first to win an Olympic medal in taekwondo at the 2008 Olympics?

39 Women's boxing bouts at the 2012 Games will be held over four rounds but how many minutes will each round last?

40 Which Olympic great has won nine gold, five silver and four bronze medals: Michael Phelps, Larisa Latynina or Carl Lewis?

41 Did the winner of the 2008 Olympic men's cycling road race take over four hours, over five hours or over six hours to complete the course?

42 Homebush Bay was the location of many of the events at which Olympic Games?

43 At the ancient Olympics *pankration* event, Sostratos of Sicyon was infamous for breaking his opponent's fingers until they surrendered: true or false?

44 Do all whitewater canoeists and kayakers at the Olympics have to wear a lifejacket called a personal flotation device?

45 For which two athletics events are throwers surrounded by a safety cage?

46 Will Hadleigh Farm host the equestrian, triathlon or mountain biking events at the 2012 Games?

47 Which European team did Cameroon defeat in the final to win gold in the 2000 Olympic men's football competition?

48 Is the long, thin competition area used in fencing called the runway, the active zone or the piste?

49 Were there over 5,000, over 8,000 or over 11,000 competitors at the 2008 Beijing Games?

50 At which Olympics was there an underwater swimming competition?

1   At the 1912 Olympics, there was a two-handed javelin competition: true or false?

2   What is the word, beginning with D, used in tennis to describe the scores in a game being level at 40-40?

3   Was volleyball originally called mintonette, bounceball or volleycourt?

4   On an athletics track, is lane eight the inside, outside or middle lane?

5   Over how many rounds is a regular Olympic taekwondo bout held?

6   At the 1900 Olympics, the 400m hurdles race used telegraph poles for hurdles and included a water jump: true or false?

7   How many barriers do hurdlers have to leap over in the men's 110m hurdles event?

8   Who became president of the International Olympic Committee in 2001: Sebastian Coe, Jacques Rogge or Juan Antonio Samaranch?

9   Did Germaine Mason, Steve Smith or Phillips Idowu win a high jump silver medal for Britain at the 2008 Olympics?

10   Which swimming stroke is the first to be swum in an Olympic team medley race?

11   In which Olympic event at the 2008 Games did the gold medallist break the world record with a height of 5.05m?

12   Which British female gymnast finished a heartbreaking 0.025 points out of the medals for the uneven bars at the 2008 Games?

13   Which country's male footballers lost their bronze medal match against Brazil at the 2008 Olympics?

14   Captain Ciaran Williams and goalkeeper Bobby White play for Great Britain in which Olympic sport?

15   Angel di Maria scored the winning goal in the final of the men's football at the 2008 Games, but for which country did he play?

16   What hurdles event is part of the men's
      Olympic decathlon?

17   Which was the second Asian nation after
      Japan to host a Summer Olympics?

18   Is the 2012 Olympic badminton
      competition taking place at the North
      Greenwich Arena, Earls Court or Wembley
      Arena?

19   In which country did the Keirin track
      cycling event originate: Japan, the United
      States, Great Britain or Italy?

20   What word, beginning with the letter A,
      is used to describe the fourth and final
      runner in a relay race?

21   In which sport did Italian Edoardo
      Mangiarotti win an extraordinary six gold,
      five silver and two bronze medals?

22   Was rhythmic gymnastics introduced at
      the 1960, 1976, 1984 or 1992 Olympics?

23   How many cyclists compete in a team
      sprint race?

24 Which Olympics was the first to feature television: 1936, 1948, 1956 or 1964?

25 In which Olympics did Tirunesh Dibaba make the Olympic record of 29 minutes 54.66 seconds for the women's 10,000m?

26 Which London park will host the show jumping event at the 2012 Olympics: Hyde Park, Greenwich Park, Victoria Park or Windsor Park?

27 How many field athletics events take place inside a throwing circle?

28 How many rounds of voting were needed for London to be selected as the host of the 2012 Games: one, two, three or four?

29 How many minutes long are women's judo bouts at the Olympics?

30 Spiridon Louis was the first winner of an Olympic: marathon, 100m sprint, long jump or shot put?

31 How many countries won just one bronze medal at the 2008 Olympics?

32 Can you name the only two things included in the gymnastic routines of both male and female gymnasts?

33 Apart from Sir Chris Hoy, which other British cyclist won more than one gold medal at the 2008 Olympics?

34 Chantal Petitclerc won a staggering fourteen gold medals in wheelchair track racing events at four Paralympics. Is she from Portugal, the United States, France or Canada?

35 In three-day eventing, how many rounds of show jumping do competitors perform along with the cross-country ride and dressage?

36 Which swimming sport is for women only at the Olympics?

37 Francisco Boza has appeared at seven Olympic Games for which country: Peru, Portugal, Honduras or Tunisia?

38 In which Olympics field athletics sport do women achieve greater distances than men?

39 From which country were the two men who have both won the Olympic heavy-weight boxing competition three times in a row?

40 Track cycling has been a part of all Olympics except one where the hosts could not build a velodrome. Which Olympics was that?

41 Which female athletics event arrived at the Olympics last out of javelin, hammer throw, 5,000m and triple jump?

42 Judo made its debut at which Paralympics: Seoul 1988, Barcelona 1992 or Atlanta 1996?

43 Was the first Olympic football competition held in 1900, 1928, 1948 or 1966?

44 In which Australian state was the 2000 Olympics held: Queensland, Victoria, Western Australia or New South Wales?

45 Which London park will see the start and finish of the triathlon competitions at the 2012 Games?

46   What is the name given to the track cycling event where riders ride behind a motorised bike called a derny for the first five and a half laps of the eight lap race?

47   Which Olympic sport was part of the 1900, 1904, 1908 and 1920 Games but did not reappear until 1972?

48   In Olympic diving, how high above the water in metres is the springboard event?

49   A team cycling sprint for men was a feature of the 2008 Olympics. Did the winning team complete the three laps of the track in approximately 43, 58 or 72 seconds?

50   Outstanding US athlete Jesse Owens won four gold medals at the 1936 Olympics. Can you name two of the events he won?

1   Neroli Fairhall competed in which Olympic sport from a wheelchair during the 1984 Olympics?

2   In what event do women launch a metal sphere weighing 4kg?

3   Do competitors in a kayak use a paddle with a blade at one end or both ends?

4   In boxing at the Olympics, one boxer wears a red singlet. What colour does his or her opponent wear?

5   In which Olympic sport do teams play two halves of 45 minutes each with a referee and two assistants controlling the game?

6   Can you name two of the three countries which finished above Great Britain in the 2008 Olympic medal table?

7   At the 1996 Olympics, Marie-José Pérec completed a rare Olympic double by winning the 200m sprint and what other race?

8   David Weir is a wheelchair track athlete who has won the London Marathon three times in a row. Can you name either of the track distances he won gold in at the 2008 Olympics?

9   Which British city competed for but failed to win the right to host the 1996 Olympics?

10 Old gas pipes were used to construct part of which London 2012 venue: the Hockey Arena, the Olympic Stadium or the Lee Valley White Water Centre?

11 At the ancient Olympics, an athlete who made a false start in a race was punished by being whipped: true or false?

12 Who won the women's pole vault gold medal in both 2004 and 2008 and has broken the world record fifteen times?

13 In the Olympic 10m air pistol shooting competition, how many shots does each marksman or woman take in the qualifying round: 20, 40, 60 or 100 shots?

14   Inge Sorensen won a bronze at the 1936 Olympics in swimming, making her the youngest known individual medallist. How old was she?

15   Were the first official Paralympic Games held in Rome, London, Mexico City or Munich?

16   At which Games were women's weight-lifting events held for the first time?

17   Which were the first Olympics to be held south of the Equator?

18   Over what distance will the 2012 Olympic canoe sprint, the shortest canoeing race, be held?

19   Did Ed Moses win two Olympic gold medals in the 110m hurdles, 200m, 400m or 400m hurdles?

20   Who won the standing long jump (where the jump is made from a standing start with no run up) at three Olympics in a row?

21 Prior to the 2016 Olympics, when did rugby last feature at an Olympic Games?

22 Did Tim Brabants win an Olympic gold medal in 2008 in rowing, kayaking, sailing or fencing?

23 How many of the eight finalists of the 2008 100m men's sprint came from the United States or the Caribbean?

24 At the 2008 Olympics, a boxer won his bout if he got how many points ahead of his opponent: 10, 15, 20 or 25?

25 The current Olympic record for the men's long jump was set in: 1968, 1988 or 2008?

26 From which Olympic Games does Dame Kelly Holmes have a bronze medal?

27 Leading all-time female Olympic medal winner, Larisa Latynina competed at how many Olympics?

28 In what sport has Hungary won over 80 Olympic medals?

29 Which nation won gold, silver and bronze medals in the men's 400m hurdles at the 2008 Olympics?

30 Tadahiro Nomura won his third gold medal and Japan's 100th ever Olympic gold medal at the 2004 Games. In what sport was Nomura competing?

31 What happens if a hurdler steps out of their lane in an athletics race and into the lane of a rival hurdler?

32 In an Olympic team fencing competition, how many fencers make up each team?

33 Is Andreas Thorkildsen, the winner of the 2008 men's javelin, from Finland, Iceland, Norway or Germany?

34 The 1916 Games were cancelled due to World War I but in which European city were they to be held?

35 How many gold medals did Vitaly Scherbo win in a single day at the 1992 Olympics?

36 How many times has San Francisco hosted the Olympic Games?

37 Which one of the following London 2012 venues is temporary and will be dismantled after the Games: the Basketball Arena, the Lee Valley White Water Centre or the Aquatics Centre?

38 All seven women's weightlifting gold medals at the 2008 Olympics were won by lifters from: Africa, Asia, Europe or North America?

39 Which European country won the women's handball competition at the 1996, 2000 and 2004 Games but failed to qualify for 2008?

40 At the 2004 Olympics, did Leslie Law win a silver and a gold in eventing, show jumping or dressage?

41 At the ancient Olympics, which combat sport was part of the pentathlon competition?

42 In which athletics event did Jan Zelezny win three gold medals in a row at the 1992, 1996 and 2000 Games?

43 Which Olympic sport was invented by British soldiers in India and was originally called Poona?

44 Nikolaos Kaklamanakis lit the Olympic cauldron at the Athens 2004 opening ceremony and would go on to win a silver medal – was it in windsurfing, pistol shooting, kayaking or judo?

45 At the 2008 Olympics, did Shawn Johnson, Nastia Liukin or Beth Tweddle win the Olympic balance beam gold medal?

46 In what Olympic sport do the two competitors start in a position facing each other called *en garde*?

47 What did people who bought tickets for London 2012 also receive: a free transport ticket, an Olympic flag, a cuddly mascot or a sports drink bottle?

48 Five European countries who were involved in World War I were not invited to the 1920 Olympics. Germany was one, can you name another?

49 Which cycling event was present at the 2008 Olympics but will not be part of London 2012: the Keirin, the Madison, the team pursuit?

50 At the 1988 Olympics, how many of the medallists in the equestrian dressage competition were women?

MEDIUM QUIZ 9

1 True or false: in the 1920 Olympics cycling race, the course ran over railway crossings and riders had to wait four minutes for a train to pass?

2 How many Russian athletes finished in the top four of the women's pole vault competition in 2008?

3 David Haye won a boxing silver medal at the 2008 Olympics: true or false?

4 How many players make up a handball team on court?

5 In which year did basketball first appear at the Olympics?

6 What is the shortest hurdles race at an Olympics?

7 In which London lake will the swimming stage of the triathlon take place at the 2012 Olympics?

8 Did women's hockey make its debut at the 1948, 1960, 1980 or 1992 Olympics?

9 True or false: Edwin Moses won 122 400m hurdles races in a row from 1977 to 1987 including two Olympic finals?

10 How many times is one team allowed to touch a volleyball before it must pass over the net?

11 Karoly Takacs lost his right hand in an accident, but learned to use his left: in which event did he win Olympic gold in both 1948 and 1952?

12 Did Asafa Powell, Maurice Greene or Justin Gatlin win gold in the men's 100m sprint at the 2004 Olympics?

13 In the 2008 Games, César Cielo Filho became Brazil's first Olympic gold medallist in swimming. Did he swim freestyle, breaststroke, butterfly or backstroke?

14 Was Jacques Rogge, President of the IOC, formerly a medical surgeon, a sports commentator, a farmer or a sportswear businessman?

15 Three countries won their first ever boxing gold medal at the 2008 Olympics, two from Asia and one from the Caribbean. Can you name any of them?

16 At which Olympic Games was Valentin Loren banned from boxing for life after punching the referee in anger?

17 At the 2012 Olympics, will cyclists head over Putney, London or Tower Bridge during the cycling road race?

18 In which year was the Olympics held in Seoul, South Korea?

19 Gymnast Alexei Nemov has won more bronze medals than any other Olympian. Is his bronze medal haul four, six, eight or ten?

20 Elvan Abeylegesse won silver in both the women's 5,000m and 10,000m races at the 2008 Olympics; from which country does she come?

21 Which London 2012 Olympic venue was first opened in 1923 and then rebuilt in the 21st century?

22 Which three women's football teams from Asia took part in the 2008 Olympic competition?

23 Where were the 1980 Olympic Games held: Manchester, Madrid or Moscow?

24 The Olympic theme music for the 1984 Games was by the same man who composed the soundtracks to the movies, *Jaws, Superman, Star Wars* and *ET*. What is his name?

25 Which Olympics was the first to feature more than 10,000 competitors?

26 Birgit Prinz and Cristiane have scored the most goals in Olympic women's football matches, but from which countries do the two players come?

27 The 2008 women's tennis singles was won by Elena Dementieva with the silver and bronze also taken by tennis players from her country. What is the country?

28 How many kilometres is the longest racewalk for women at the Olympics?

29 Is the lightest weight division in men's Olympic taekwondo called lightweight, catchweight or flyweight?

30 In which sport did father and son, Bill and Wayne Roycroft, win a bronze medal in 1976 as part of the same three person team?

31 Oscar Swahn is the oldest ever Olympic competitor. He won a silver medal in what sport at the age of 72?

32 At which Olympics did canoeing and handball first appear, whilst polo made its final appearance?

33 At the 2008 Games, which country won as many cycling gold medals as the next six countries on the medal table combined?

34 Was Bob Matthias 17, 20, 23 or 39 when he won the 1948 Olympic decathlon?

35 Oussama Mellouli won the 2008 men's 1500m freestyle competition, becoming the first African to win an individual swimming event. What country is he from?

36 What did John Godina accidentally throw into the back of his US athletics team-mate during warm-up at the 1996 Olympics?

37 Which one of the following countries did not win their first Olympic medal in 1996: Mozambique, Armenia, Namibia or Uzbekistan?

38 At the 1992 Olympics, which South American country won just one bronze medal (in the men's tennis doubles)?

39 In which track athletics event did Tasha Danvers win a bronze medal at the 2008 Olympics?

40 When was the last year the Winter and Summer Olympics were held in the same country?

41 Did Japan, China, South Korea or the United States win the most judo medals at the 2008 Olympics?

42 At the 1956 Olympics, a combined Great Britain football team suffered its worst Olympic defeat. Did they lose 6-1 to Spain, Argentina, Brazil or Bulgaria?

43 Was the first women's marathon run at the 1972, 1984, 1992 or 2000 Olympics?

44 At the 1976 Olympics, over twenty countries from which continent boycotted the Games?

45 To within 5cm, how tall was the tallest ever female Olympic gold medallist, Iuliana Semenova?

46 Which two of the following do sprint bicycles used in track racing not have: gears, handlebars, brakes, saddle?

47 At the 1932 Olympics, which country thrashed the United States field hockey team 24-1?

48 In which county will the 2012 Olympic mountain biking competitions be held: Sussex, Essex, Surrey or Berkshire?

49 In what team sport did Iceland win its only medal, a silver, at the 2008 Olympics?

50 Which South American team pulled out of the 1936 Olympics after a football match featuring their team and Austria was ordered to be replayed following crowd trouble?

1   What is the only Olympic sport where competitors always cross the finishing line going backwards?

2   How many sailors will you find in a Yngling boat at the Olympics?

3   Is each game in a badminton match played to 11, 15 or 21 points?

4   Was Hank Lammens disqualified from one 1992 yachting race for: crashing his boat into another competitor's, forgetting his lifejacket or fitting a secret motor to his yacht?

5   Which Scottish stadium will host Olympic football at the 2012 Games?

6   At the 1976 Olympics, brothers Leon and Michael Spinks both won gold medals, but in which sport?

7   Can you name the two track events in a women's Olympic pentathlon competition?

8   How many laps of the track do athletes run to complete the 10,000m?

9   At the 2004 Olympics, was 750 litres of tomato sauce used to make food every hour, every day or every week?

10 At the 2008 Olympics, Natalia Partyka, born without a right hand, took part in which Olympic sport: diving, badminton, softball or table tennis?

11 Which small European nation, whose name starts and ends with the same letter, boycotted four Olympics in a row (1976-1988)?

12 Can you name one of the cycling events that Chris Hoy won at the 2008 Olympics?

13 Félix Savon won boxing gold medals at three Olympics in a row but at what weight?

14 Was the 400m individual medley, the 100m freestyle or the 200m butterfly the first event in which Michael Phelps won an Olympic gold?

15 How many points is a bullseye in archery worth?

16 Blanka Vlasic and Tia Hellebaut both cleared 2.05m in the 2008 women's high jump, but which jumper won because she made fewer failed attempts in the competition?

17 At the Moscow Olympics in 1980, did female competitors make up 20%, 35%, 50% or 60% of all competitors?

18 In wheelchair tennis at the Paralympics, how many times is the ball allowed to bounce on a player's side of the court?

19 Can you name either of the cities, beginning with the letter M, that London beat to host the 2012 Olympics?

20 At London 2012, will the women's cycling road race be over a course approximately 60km, 90km, 130km or 150km long?

21 In which athletics event did Iolanda Balas win two Olympic gold medals in the 1960s as well as going unbeaten in 140 competitions in a row?

22 For which Olympic Games did EMI release an official pop and rock music album called *Unity*, featuring Moby, Destiny's Child and Sting amongst others?

23 Which country won all three medals in the men's two-handed javelin at the 1912 Olympics?

24 Which of these was an Olympic sport in 1900: darts, snooker, croquet or bowls?

25 How many Olympic Games featured polo on horseback as a medal event?

26 Did women's wheelchair rugby become a medal sport at the 1992, 2000 or 2008 Paralympic Games?

27 Who is the only person to be the Olympic record holder in three athletics events?

28 How many Olympic gold medals did kayak racing star Birgit Fischer win during her career?

29 In Olympic three position rifle shooting, can you name two of the three positions shooters must fire in?

30 Which Scandinavian country's flag wasn't displayed at the 1908 London Olympic stadium, causing that country's team to pull out of the opening ceremony?

31 James Connolly took part in the long jump, high jump and triple jump at the 1896 Olympics. Which event did he win a gold medal in?

32 At the 1992 Olympics, Sammy Kuffour became the youngest men's Olympic football medallist when his team, Ghana, won bronze. How old was Kuffour?

33 Was the long jump for women added to the Olympics in 1928, 1948 or 1968?

34 How many different coloured cards do the umpires in a hockey game use to warn or punish players?

35 Up to the 2012 Olympics, Iran has won 48 medals but in only three different sports. Can you name two of them?

36 Did the men's discus throw first appear at the 1896, 1908 or 1920 Olympics?

37 At the 1912 Olympics, how long did a single wrestling bout between Martin Klein and Alfred Asikainen last: 4 hours 20 minutes, 6 hours 10 minutes, 8 hours 30 minutes or 11 hours 40 minutes?

38 Cassius Marcellus Clay won a boxing gold medal at the 1960 Olympics. Who is he better known as?

39 Birgit Fischer won her first gold medal at the 1980 Olympics. At which Olympics did she win her last?

40 How long did boxing contests at the ancient Olympics last: 10 minutes, 30 minutes, 60 minutes or for as long as both men were still standing?

41 Were the 1928 Olympics held in New York, Amsterdam, Melbourne or Rome?

42 The Olympic record for the women's 4x100m athletics relay was set by a country which is now part of a different nation. Can you name it?

43 In tennis, what score in a set causes the set to go into a tiebreaker?

44 How many Olympic gold medals did Carl Lewis win in sprinting and the long jump?

45 Did synchronised swimming first appear as an Olympic competition at Los Angeles, Seoul, Barcelona or Atlanta?

46 In the Olympic motto, does the word 'citius' mean higher, more powerful or faster?

47 In the Paralympics, would a field athletics competitor classified as F41 be: an amputee, a wheelchair athlete or visually impaired?

48 Which European city was supposed to host the 1908 Olympics before a volcanic eruption saw it moved to London?

49 Daley Thompson celebrated his gold medal in the decathlon by taking a bath filled with wine instead of water: true or false?

50 Which country's relay runners were amongst the favourites to win both the men's and women's 4x100m relay at the 2008 Olympics but in both competitions dropped the baton and failed to reach the final?

WINTER OLYMPICS QUIZ 2

1 Rhona Martin captained which British Winter Olympics sport's team in 2006?

2 In a qualifying game for the 2010 Olympics, which European men's ice hockey team, beginning with the letter S, beat Bulgaria 82-0?

3 How many times has the Winter Olympics been held in Asia?

4 How many countries sent athletes to compete at the 2010 Winter Olympics: 23, 41, 67 or 82?

5 Charles Jewtraw became the first Winter Olympic gold medallist in 1924 but was his event: downhill skiing, speed skating or men's luge?

6 How many stones does a curling team propel in one end of curling?

7 Can you name either one of the two countries, whose name begins with the letter P, which made their Winter Olympic debut in 2010?

8   The 1998 Nagano Olympics featured four mascots, Sukki, Nokki, Lekki and Tsukki. What type of bird were they?

9   Which sport appeared at the 1920 Summer Olympics and the 1924 Winter Olympics?

10   Britain's Amy Williams won what medal at the 2010 Olympics in the skeleton?

11   Which bobsleigh made its first Olympic appearance in 2002; the four man, two man, four woman or two woman?

12   Which Asian nation won six gold medals in speed skating at the 2006 Olympics?

13   Did 11, 86, 124 or 219 women take part in the first Winter Olympics?

14   Which British skier won a medal at the 2002 Winter Olympics but was later disqualified for using a nasal inhaler for colds which contained a banned substance?

15 At the 2010 Games, did each competitor in the men's biathlon relay ski 5km, 7.5km, 10km or 15km?

16 Lillehammer hosted the 1994 Winter Games: in which country is it located?

17 What event was held outdoors for the last time at the 1956 Olympics?

18 Christa Rothenburger won a silver in the women's sprint cycling at the 1988 Olympics but in which sport did she win a silver and gold at the Winter Olympics in the same year?

19 Which Scandinavian country knocked out Great Britain's men's curling team at the semi-final stage of the 2006 Games?

20 How many snowboarders take part in the final of the half pipe competition?

21 Seth Wescott won gold in 2006 and 2010 in the same event: what was it?

22 Which country, that no longer exists, won the men's biathlon relay at six Olympics in a row (1968-1988)?

23 At which Olympics did Diana Gordon-Lennox ski the downhill course wearing a monocle, a plaster cast on her arm and using only one pole?

24 Sapporo hosted the 1972 Winter Games, but in which country is it located?

25 39-year-old Duff Gibson became the oldest individual Winter Olympic gold medallist in 2006 when he won which event: skeleton, 20km biathlon, men's figure skating or 500m speed skating?

26 Were the 2006 Winter Olympics held in Salt Lake City, Chamonix or Turin?

27 Which two countries won three snowboarding gold medals each at the 2006 Olympics?

28 At which Games did Eric Heiden compete in five different speed-skating events, winning them all?

29 Can you name one of the three countries which won medals in the women's biathlon relay in both 2006 and 2010?

30 How many medals did Great Britain win at the 2006 Winter Olympics?

31 Is Olympic champion snowboarder Shaun White's nickname the Flying Tomato, the Swooping Carrot or the Ginger Ninja?

32 How many riders take part in each race of Olympic snowboard cross?

33 In which Olympic sport is the individual event held over 15km for women and 20km for men?

34 Chemmy Alcott made her Winter Olympic debut at the 2002 Games, in what sport?

35 How many runs down the track do individual competitors make in the Olympic luge event?

36 Two Winter Olympics have been held in countries which no longer exist. Can you name either country?

37 Can you name either of the two countries, whose names begin with the letter C, which made their Winter Olympics debut in 2010?

38 Does each curling stone weigh 4.4kg, 7.2kg, 13.3kg or 19.1kg?

39 What was the name of the film loosely based on the Jamaican bobsleigh team which entered the 1988 Winter Olympics?

40 Finland's Raimo Ilmari Helminen is the only person to appear at six Winter Olympics in which sport?

41 In what Winter Olympics event did Eddie 'The Eagle' Edwards compete in 1988?

42 Which country, beginning with the letter A, has won 201 Winter Olympic medals up to and including Vancouver 2010?

43 The Bolshoi Ice Palace will host the final of which sport at the 2014 Winter Olympics?

44 Which US skier overslept on the morning of the men's downhill skiing competition and ended up finishing in fifth place?

45 How long did ski jumper Anders Haugen have to wait to receive his Olympic medal, not awarded at the 1924 Games due to a scoring mistake?

46 Was the first ever Winter Olympics held in Chamonix, Lake Placid, Innsbruck or Lillehammer?

47 What piece of music by Ravel did Torville and Dean dance to when winning Olympic gold?

48 Which American city won the right to host the 1976 Winter Olympics but its residents refused and the competition was held in Innsbruck, Austria instead?

49 What was the longest distance race Eric Heiden won Olympic gold in?

50 Simon Ammann won his fourth ski jump gold medal in 2010. In the large hill event, can you guess how far his two jumps equalled (to the nearest 10m)?

1   How long is the longest swimming race at the 2012 Olympics?

2   Do you sit, kneel or stand when racing in an Olympic canoe?

3   In 2006, which city finally paid off the last of its debts from hosting the Olympic Games?

4   Since 2011, does a modern pentathlon end with a 10km cycling race, a 200m swimming race or a combined shooting competition and 3,000m cross-country run?

5   What sort of Australian animal was the Sydney 2000 mascot, Syd?

6   At how many Olympic Games did javelin thrower Tessa Sanderson appear?

7   In which famous football stadium will the opening and closing ceremonies of the 2016 Olympics take place: Wembley, the San Siro, the Maracana or Soccer City?

8   How many sailors race in each Finn class sailing dinghy?

9   Is the name of one of the London 2012 mascots: Linford, Mandelson, Wenlock or Jackson?

10 At the 2004 Olympics, Hicham El Guerrouj won the 1,500m and which other track athletics race?

11 Which American city did London beat to host the 2012 Games?

12 Which women's basketball team has won three Olympic silver medals in a row having been beaten by the United States in all three finals?

13 More than 250,000 tourists visit the official Olympic museum every year – but what Swiss city is it located in?

14 In the 1936 Olympic long jump competition, which German rival of Jesse Owens gave him advice and finished with silver behind him?

15 Which of the apparatus used by rhythmic gymnasts begins with the letter H?

16 Did Cuba, Russia, Germany or France win the women's volleyball competition at three Olympics in a row (1992-2000)?

17 Were the 1920 Olympics held in Antwerp, Rome, Madrid or Berlin?

18 At the Atlanta Olympics were there three million, seven million or eleven million tickets available?

19 Did Tony Blair, Sir Steve Redgrave, David Cameron or Boris Johnson receive the Olympic flag from the mayor of Beijing at the 2008 Olympics?

20 How many times do steeplechasers have to leap the water jump in a 3,000m race?

21 How old was Carlos Front when he was the cox in the Spanish rowing eight at the 1992 Olympics?

22 Ian Millar has appeared at more Olympics than any other equestrian competitor. Has he competed in three, five, seven or nine Olympic Games?

23 Zhang Yining won both individual and team Olympic gold medals at the 2004 and 2008 Olympics, but in what sport?

24 Welles Hoyt's performance was measured at 3.30 metres when he won which athletics event at the 1896 Olympics: long jump, high jump, rope climb or pole vault?

25 Which one of the following locations is not part of the 2012 Olympic torch relay: The Orkneys, the Isle of Wight, the Shetlands, the Isle of Man, Jersey, or Guernsey?

26 Simon Whitfield from Canada was the first men's Olympic gold medallist in which sport?

27 Will the London 2012 Olympic Stadium hold a maximum of 65,000, 80,000, 90,000 or 105,000 spectators?

28 In 2004, who was the first British woman to win two athletics gold medals at a single Olympics?

29 Where were the 1972 Games held?

30 Runners from the same African nation have won the last seven men's Olympic 3,000m steeplechase gold medals. Which country is it?

31 Which sport on the water was added to the 2008 Paralympics?

32 Which famous heavyweight world champion boxer (who would later have part of his ear bitten off by Mike Tyson in a fight) was disqualified from the 1984 Olympics for knocking his opponent out after the referee had told the boxers to break?

33 Angel Matos was banned for life from taekwondo after attacking a referee at which Olympics?

34 Did the martial art of taekwondo originate in Korea, Japan or Thailand?

35 In 2008, Abhinav Bindra became the first ever individual gold medallist for which country?

36 How many attempts at lifting a particular weight does a weightlifter get at an Olympics?

37 If you were in the peloton, but looking to attack and make a breakaway, would you be cycling, playing handball or swimming a relay race?

38 Less than half of the London Underground tube system that will be used by visitors in 2012 is actually underground: true or false?

39 Abebe Bikila won the 1960 Olympic men's marathon: wearing hobnail boots, after having to change trainers or in bare feet?

40 How many gold medals did Tanni Gray win at the 1992 Olympics for Great Britain: two, three, four or five?

41 In which two athletics events is a strip of modelling clay placed on the take-off board to check that athletes don't overstep?

42 At the 1980 Olympics, two female gymnasts both scored the same for their floor routine and were both awarded gold medals. Nellie Kim was one of the pair, who was the other?

43 On the 2004 Olympic torch relay, what was the last country, beginning with C, the torch visited before returning to Greece?

44 For how many Olympics did baseball appear as a medal sport before being discontinued after 2008?

45 Was Nellie Kim, Nadia Comaneci, Mary Lou Retton or Olga Korbut the first gymnast to perform a backward somersault on the balance beam?

46 Can you name two of the four field athletics events in a women's Olympic heptathlon competition?

47 At which Olympics did world-famous boxer Muhammad Ali light the Olympic flame during the opening ceremony?

48 In whitewater canoeing, a penalty of how many seconds is added to a competitor's time if they touch a gate pole?

49 At the 2004 Olympics, which country won more bronze medals (38) than any other nation?

50 Which country's athletes were so penniless when arriving for the 1932 Olympics that many of them sold coffee to make a living?

 MEDIUM QUIZ 12

1 At which Olympics did the Duke of Edinburgh perform the opening ceremony?

2 What is the maximum number of people in a boat in the Olympic rowing events?

3 You are allowed to grip below the hips and use your legs in which form of wrestling: Greco-Roman or Freestyle?

4 In Olympic boxing, what weight division is found between light welterweight and featherweight?

5 In which cycling event do riders wear full face helmets and ride bikes with small (51cm diameter) wheels?

6   Manuel Estiarte appeared at six Olympic Games, in four of which he was the tournament's highest scorer, but in which sport: hockey, handball, volleyball or water polo?

7   In 1952, what travelled by air for the first time?

8   Which bird's feathers are said to make the best shuttlecocks used in badminton?

9   Which is the lightest fencing weapon: foil, sabre or épée?

10   Were there over 2,000, over 4,000, over 7,000 or over 9,000 competitors at the 1972 Olympics?

11   Who won the 2008 gold medal in the women's pole vault: Yelena Isinbayeva, Kelly Sotherton or Monika Pyrek?

12   What day of the week will the 2012 closing ceremony be held on?

13   Can you name any of the four events in which Fanny Blankers-Koen won gold medals at the 1948 Olympics?

14 Which one of the following did not win a basketball gold medal with the USA team in 2008: Dwight Howard, LeBron James, Kobe Bryant or Kevin Garnett?

15 The 1960 women's discus champion, Elvira Ozolina, was so unhappy with herself for coming fifth in 1964 that she: jumped into a cold pond, shaved her head or gave away her 1960 gold medal?

16 At the 1992 Olympics, which small island nation finished above Great Britain, Australia, France and Japan in the medal table?

17 Do the archers stand 20m, 35m, 55m or 70m away from their targets?

18 Who won an amazing 18 Olympics medals throughout her career?

19 In which Olympic sport are different grips called pen-hold and shakehands?

20 At which Olympics did Michael Johnson and Marie-José Pérec each win both their 200m and 400m athletics races?

21 Did the winner of the women's BMX competition at the 2008 Olympics complete the course in under 36 seconds, under 56 seconds or under 1 minute 16 seconds?

22 How many different badminton events are there at the 2012 Olympics?

23 Which Olympic sport is to be hosted at Earls Court during the 2012 Games?

24 At which Olympics was Cobi the dog the mascot: Barcelona, Los Angeles, Munich or Sydney?

25 Tragedy struck at the 1960 Olympics when Knud Jensen died. In which sport was he competing?

26 At which Summer Olympic Games did Britain not win a single bronze medal?

27 Which film director is in charge of the 2012 Olympics opening ceremony?

28 What sort of Australian bird was the Sydney 2000 mascot, Olly?

29 At the 2004 Olympics, Bryan Lomas, the smallest competitor, took part in which sport?

30 Is the London 2012 dressage competition to be held in Hyde Park, St James's Park or Greenwich Park?

31 What was the one new athletics track event included in the 2008 Olympics?

32 Which individual ball sport will be newly included in the Olympics in 2016?

33 How many running events are there in a modern pentathlon?

34 Lacrosse was included in which two of the following Games: Paris, St Louis, London or Stockholm?

35 Did Birgit Prinz, Carli Lloyd or Shannon Boxx score the winning goal in the 2008 Olympic women's football final?

36 In which Olympic sport do the best competitors perform Quadriffis – a twist with four complete somersaults?

37 At the 1956 Olympics, two water polo teams fought in the pool so much they turned the pool's water red with blood. Can you name either team?

38 Trischa Zorn won over 40 medals in blind swimming events at how many Paralympic Games?

39 At which weight did boxer Cassius Clay win Olympic gold: welterweight, light-heavyweight or heavyweight?

40 At the 1900 Olympics the Danish-Swedish team was a man short and asked a journalist to join in, going on to win the gold medal – in which event?

41 Which former European country's men's volleyball team beat Russia to win the 2000 Olympic competition?

42 Was the 1972 Paralympic Games held in Munich, Heidelberg, Paris or Berlin?

43 Great Britain's men's basketball star Luo Deng plays in the NBA for which team: Chicago Bulls, LA Lakers or San Antonio Spurs?

44 Aladar Gerevich is the only athlete in any sport to have won the same Olympic event six times. Was his sport fencing, badminton, the hammer throw or heavyweight weightlifting?

45 The men's individual pursuit track cycling race was held at the Olympics from 1964 to 2008. Was it 3,000m, 4,000m or 5,000m long?

46 One of the stars of the 1912 Games, Jim Thorpe, had to return his Olympic medals after it was discovered that he had played which American sport at semi-professional level?

47 Alexandra Schreiber lost her 1992 Olympic judo bout in 7, 27 or 47 seconds?

48 Before the 1984 Olympics what was the longest track race for female athletes at the Olympics?

49 At the 1976 Olympics, Japan's Shun Fujimoto broke his kneecap but continued to compete, helping his team win gold, in what Olympic sport?

50 Joan Benoit was the winner of the first women's Olympic marathon but was she from France, Canada or the USA?

MEDIUM QUIZ 13

1 Can you name four of the five colours of the rings on the Olympic flag?

2 Was the 200m athletics race held in a straight line with no bend to run, in 1904, 1912, 1924 or 1932?

3 Mark Hunter and Zac Purchase together won a gold medal at the 2008 Games in which sport: cycling, rowing, sailing or badminton doubles?

4 In which event at the 1932 Olympics did the officials make the athletes run an extra lap by mistake?

5 At the 2000 Olympics, can you name the sport beginning with the letter W, that women did not take part in?

6. Jeff Float won a swimming gold medal in the pool at the 1984 Olympics: true or false?

7. In Olympic boxing is welterweight lighter or heavier than lightweight?

8. Did women's judo become a medal sport at the 1984, 1992 or 2000 Olympics?

9. What was the last Olympics to feature baseball as a medal sport?

10. Was the most expensive ticket at the 2012 Olympics for the opening ceremony, the 100m final or the final of the gymnastics?

11. Is Jacques Rogge the 8th, 14th, 23rd or 34th President of the IOC?

12. At the 2012 Games, only two stadiums used for the football events are Premier League grounds. Can you name both?

13. Can you name the two Olympic sports, both beginning with the letter B, which women could not take part in at the 2000 Games?

14   What number does a referee count to in order to count a boxer out of the fight?

15   How many Olympic silver medals has Michael Phelps won?

16   At which Olympics did a terrorist attack kill eleven athletes and coaches from Israel and a West German police officer?

17   An East German team set an Olympic record in 1980 that has yet to be beaten. Was the sport 4x400m swimming, 4x100m running or team gymnastics?

18   Which one of the following will be added to the 2012 Olympics: skateboarding, tennis mixed doubles or rugby sevens?

19   Which was the first city to host the Olympic Games twice?

20   Which swimmer was banned from competing for ten years after trying to steal an Olympic flag as a prank at the 1964 Olympics?

21 In what sport did Jacques Rogge compete in three Olympics before becoming President of the International Olympic Committee?

22 At the ancient Olympics, what was a *kotinos*: a crown of olive leaves given to winners, a large jug of olive oil used by athletes before competing or the name given to an athlete's personal coach?

23 Synchronised swimming competitions for single swimmers appeared at how many Olympics before it was discontinued?

24 From what country does 2008 110m hurdles Olympic champion, Dayron Robles come?

25 What type of fencing event is part of the modern pentathlon: sabre, foil or épée?

26 What was the name given to the new technique for clearing the high jump bar head-first, pioneered by Dick Fosbury?

27 Which Olympic sport was founded by Jigoro Kano in Tokyo?

28 Which nation is the only country to have won over 1,000 Olympic gold medals?

29 After some runners were exhausted at the end of the women's 800m in 1928, when was the women's 800m next seen at the Olympics?

30 At the 2004 Games in Athens, which athletics field event was held at Olympia?

31 Which famous clothes maker won a bronze medal in men's doubles tennis at the 1924 Olympics: Fred Perry, René Lacoste or Vivienne Westwood?

32 Are 1,000, 3,000, 5,000 or 8,000 people expected to carry the 2012 Olympic torch on its relay?

33 Did Sarah Stevenson win a 2008 taekwondo bronze medal in the flyweight, lightweight or heavyweight division?

34 French concert pianist Micheline Ostermeyer won gold in which two field athletics events at the 1948 Olympics?

35 In which cycling event does any rider who is lapped by another have to leave the race?

36 How many riders make up a cycling pursuit team?

37 Can you name two of the five London boroughs that are hosting the London 2012 Olympics?

38 How wide is the discus throwing circle at an Olympic Games?

39 In which Olympic sport did ancient Olympic competitors wear leather straps wrapped around their hands instead of gloves?

40 Do you have to weigh over 80, over 90 or over 100kg to take part in the men's heavy-weight judo competition at the Olympics?

41 In 1984, the Paralympics were split into two locations for financial reasons. Part of the Games were held in Stoke Mandeville in Britain; in which American city were the remainder held?

42   Luis Scola scored 37 points, the most in a single basketball game by any player at the 2008 Olympics, but was he playing against Latvia, Russia, the USA or Spain?

43   Was Yelena Isinbayeva, Stacy Dragila or Jennifer Suhr the first female pole vaulter to clear a height of over five metres?

44   Gabriel Minadeo Ramírez competed for the Argentinian men's team in this sport in three Olympics in a row before he coached the Argentinian women's Olympic team in 2008. What is the sport?

45   At which Olympics did gold, silver and bronze medals feature the semi-precious stone, jade?

46   Which famous athlete won the 1936 Olympic men's long jump a year after making a world record jump that wasn't beaten for 25 years?

47   Was Lori Fung the first Olympic champion at women's weightlifting, women's pole vault, women's table tennis or rhythmic gymnastics?

48 Every male member of the GB Olympic team in 1948 was given one free item of clothing. Was it a pair of underpants, an overcoat, a tracksuit or a pinstripe suit?

49 Which country's football players became the first female Olympic football champions?

50 What is the name of the piece of gymnastics apparatus on legs with two semi-circular handles on its top?

 MEDIUM QUIZ 14

1 At which Olympic Games was the mascot an eagle called Sam?

2 How many gymnasts take part in a team rhythmic gymnastics performance at the Olympics?

3 Which swimming stroke is the first to be swum in an Olympic Individual Medley race?

4   At what famous tennis venue will the 2012 Olympic tennis competition be held?

5   What type of medal did boxer, Amir Khan win at the 2004 Olympics?

6   How many kilometres long is the run at the end of the triathlon?

7   In which soon to be Olympic sport do players drive, chip and putt to try to score birdies and eagles?

8   How many Olympics were cancelled due to World War I and World War II?

9   In which year was the Olympics first held in London?

10   What city were the Olympics held in when the USA team boycotted them in protest?

11   In 1906, the International Olympic Committee held a ten-year anniversary competition called the Intercalated Games which is not normally counted in Olympic histories and statistics. Where was the event held?

12 Who ran barefoot in the 1984 Olympic 3,000m final, tangling with Mary Decker who fell?

13 Bob Mathias took up which athletics event just four months before winning the 1948 Olympic gold medal?

14 At the 2000 Olympics torch relay, the Olympic flame was carried in a special waterproof container underwater through which famous reef?

15 At which Olympics would you have seen Chris Boardman win gold on a revolutionary new superbike with wheels made of solid discs?

16 Is the men's Olympic marathon record under 127 minutes, under 140 minutes or under 155 minutes?

17 In which Olympic sport is Canada's Karen Cockburn the only competitor to win a medal at three Olympics in a row (2000 to 2008)?

18 Which US gymnast fell into the judges after a vault went wrong during the 2004 men's competition, but recovered to win the gold medal in the all around competition: Paul Hamm, Blaine Wilson or Morgan Hamm?

19 Did the women's modern pentathlon make its first Olympic appearance at the Munich, Seoul, Atlanta or Sydney Games?

20 In 2004, Gal Friedman won Israel's first ever Olympic gold medal – in which sport?

21 Who won the 2008 Olympics baseball gold medal: USA, Japan, France or South Korea?

22 At the 1984 Olympics, Carrie Steinseifer and Nancy Hogshead both swam the same time (55.92 seconds) and both received a gold medal in which event: 50m butterfly, 100m freestyle, 50m backstroke or 100m breaststroke?

23 How many players are there in a softball team?

24 Which country appeared at the 1992 Olympics, their first since 1960?

25 Which two of the following are films by the director of the 2012 Olympics opening ceremony: *Slumdog Millionaire, The King's Speech, 28 Days Later, Chariots of Fire?*

26 What was the name given to the five-event competition held at the ancient Olympics?

27 Which country's female archers have won eleven individual or team gold medals since 1984?

28 Can you name two of the four cities London beat to host the 2012 Olympics?

29 Trooping of the Colour is a parade involving Queen Elizabeth II travelling from Buckingham Palace to a parade ground which will host the 2012 Olympic beach volleyball competition. What is the parade ground called?

30 How many Olympics featured softball as a medal sport: three, four, five or six?

31 When road cycle racing legend Jeannie Longo competed at the 2008 Games, was it her fourth, fifth, sixth or seventh Olympics in a row?

32 The oldest competitor at the 2008 Olympics was 67-year-old Hiroshi Hoketsu. Did he compete in archery, equestrianism, sailing or fencing?

33 At the 1992 Olympics, the US men's basketball team won all its matches. Did they have an average winning margin of 13, 23, 33 or 43 points more than their opponents?

34 Eton Manor will be the venue for what 2012 Paralympics event: wheelchair tennis, blind football, wheelchair rugby or Paralympic archery?

35 Was 4kg, 33kg, 98kg or 1,000kg of silver needed to make all the gold and silver medals at the 2004 Olympics?

36 Which Olympic athletics event first appeared at the ancient Olympics in 708 BCE when it featured an implement made of stone and bronze?

37 Were the first Olympic shooting events for women held at the 1984, 1992 or 2004 Olympics?

38 Gold medals have been awarded to winners of events at every modern Olympic Games: true or false?

39 Abhinav Bindra won his country's first ever individual gold medal at the 2008 Olympics. What was his sport?

40 Was the 2008 women's long jump champion, Maurren Higa Maggi, from Brazil, Italy, Australia or Belgium?

41 What is the name given to the lightest weight division in Olympic taekwondo?

42 Which one of the following did three-time athletics gold medallist, Wilma Rudolph, not suffer from as a child: tuberculosis, scarlet fever, whooping cough or polio?

43 In which city did the 4x100m relay for men make its Olympic debut?

44 Which British javelin thrower won the bronze medal in 1992 and silver medals in 1996 and 2000?

45 Paralympic track athletes classified as T12: are visually impaired, are in a wheelchair or have cerebral palsy?

46 What was the name of the founder of the modern Olympic Games?

47 Which famous palace, west of London and once the home of King Henry VIII, will road cyclists cycle past during the 2012 Olympics?

48 What did Sweden's Anders Ahlgren and Finland's Ivan Bohling receive after wrestling for over nine hours with neither winning their 1912 Olympic bout?

49 What was the name of Cian O'Connor's horse which tested positive for banned drugs and was disqualified from the 2004 Olympics: Giddy Up Boy, Helios, Schaffer II or Waterford Crystal?

50 Can you name either of the two mascots at the 2004 Olympics?

MEDIUM QUIZ 15

1 Which country won the most gold medals, 51, at the 2008 Olympics?

2 In which event did Britain win its only field athletics medal at the 2008 Olympics?

3 Does the platform divers use in Olympic platform diving stand 3m, 6m, 10m or 12m above the water?

4 At the 2008 Olympics which country's 4x200m men's relay swimming team became the first ever to swim under seven minutes?

5 Which country has won 40 cycling gold medals, more than any other nation?

6 Tokyo held the Olympics in 1964 but in which year were they originally planned to host the Games, only for World War II to cause them to be cancelled?

7   When handball debuted at the Olympics, did each team play with one, two, three or four players more than teams play with now?

8   Germany came second in the 1904 Olympic medal table but was its tally 18, 42, 68 or 226 medals behind the United States?

9   Almudena Cid Tostado is the only competitor to reach the rhythmic gymnastics Olympic final four times in a row. Which four Olympics?

10   Who was the mayor of London when the city won the right to host the 2012 Olympics?

11   Which small European nation's men's basketball team has finished third or fourth in the last five Olympics?

12   According to the official schedule, which Olympic multi-sport event will be the last to finish at London 2012, just 90 minutes before the closing ceremony?

13 Which stadium will be the most northerly venue used for the London 2012 Olympics?

14 Where is the 2004 decathlon gold medallist Roman Šebrle from: the Ukraine, Italy, the Czech Republic or Romania?

15 When was the last time tennis mixed doubles appeared at the Olympics before 2012?

16 Heavyweight boxer Lennox Lewis was born in West Ham, close to the 2012 Olympic Park, but which country did he represent when he won a 1988 Olympic gold medal?

17 Of the eighteen medals awarded in the past six Olympics in the men's 10,000m race, how many have gone to someone from outside Africa?

18 At the 2004 Olympics, spectator Cornelius Horan ran out onto the course to wrestle the race leader, Vanderlei de Lima. What race was taking place?

19   In what position did Vanderlei de Lima eventually finish the above race?

20   In the ancient Olympics, a race for hoplites was introduced around 520 BCE. Were hoplites: men wearing 25kg of armour, women carrying jars of olive oil or sons and daughters of wealthy ancient Greeks?

21   Afanasijs Kuzmins has appeared at eight Olympics. Was he taking part in archery, fencing, shooting or badminton events?

22   At the 1896 Olympics, Carl Schuhmann won the heavyweight Greco-Roman wrestling competition. Schuhmann also took part in three other sports at that Olympics. Can you name two of them?

23   In which event at the 2008 Olympics did Sherone Simpson and Kerron Stewart both finish with the exact same time and win silver medals?

24   Lisa Leslie and Teresa Edwards are the two basketball players with the most Olympic gold medals. How many?

25 Did an Australian teenager, a French politician, a member of the British Royal Family or a famous American swimmer come up with the idea of a closing ceremony at the end of the Olympics?

26 Was the first Olympic stadium in London: Wembley Stadium, White City Stadium, Stamford Bridge or White Hart Lane?

27 What multi-sport athletics event for women was held between 1964 and 1980 before it was superseded by the heptathlon?

28 Millions of visitors will use the world famous London Underground map when visiting during 2012; did its designer, Harry Beck, earn just over £5, £500, £5,000 or £500,000 for designing it?

29 The first competitive event of the 2012 Olympics is held at 4pm on July 25th, at which British stadium?

30 With which famous rower did Steve Redgrave win his last Olympic rowing gold medal?

31 At which Olympics was a fake Olympic flame made out of old underpants handed to the mayor of the city as a student prank – 1956, 1968 or 1992?

32 Did the modern pentathlon for men make its first Olympic appearance at London, Stockholm, Paris or Los Angeles?

33 If all the Olympic sports were listed alphabetically, which would be the first on the list?

34 Eleven different cities entered bidding to host the 2004 Olympics won by Athens. Can you name one of the four which begin with the letter S?

35 During the 2008 Olympics, were four, eight, ten or thirteen men's Olympic records in athletics broken?

36 German Friedrich Traun won the men's doubles tennis at the 1896 Olympics but from what other European country was his partner, John Pius Boland?

37 How many medals did Great Britain win at the 2008 Olympics: 13, 24, 31 or 47?

38 Which country won both the men's and women's team artistic gymnastics competitions at the 2008 Olympics: China, the United States, Russia or Romania?

39 Have one, three, five or seven athletes won both the 800m and 1,500m track races at a single Olympics?

40 Great Britain's David Davies won which medal in the first 10km open water swim competition held at an Olympics?

41 At the 2008 Olympics, which Ethiopian woman won gold in both the 5,000m and 10,000m athletics races?

42 Tuvalu's sole athlete at the 2008 Olympics, track sprinter Asenate Manoa, used to train on Tuvalu's airport runway: true or false?

43 How many Olympic medals did Sebastian Coe win as a middle distance runner?

44 What is the name, beginning with the letter M, of one of the two London 2012 official mascots?

45 No women took part in the first modern Olympics in 1896: true or false?

46 The 1948 London Olympics was held on a shoestring with contributions from other countries. Which European country donated 160,000 eggs to feed athletes?

47 At the 1896 Olympics, Dimitrios Loundras was just 10 years and 218 days old when his team came second in what sport: gymnastics, swimming relay or archery?

48 Will the arena hosting the water polo competition at the 2012 Games hold 1,500, 5,000, 12,000 or 26,000 spectators?

49 What did Olympic long distance running champion, Paavo Nurmi, often carry in his hand as he raced?

50 Whilst the body of Baron de Coubertin, the founder of the Olympic Games, was buried in Switzerland, what part of his body was removed and buried in Greece?

1. Who fell during the 1972 final of the 10,000m, picked himself up from the track and went on to win gold?

2. In Usain Bolt's astonishing 100m victory at the 2008 Olympics, who came second?

3. Which is the only Olympic sport at London 2012 where women and men will compete directly against each other?

4. How many Olympic gold medals in long distance running events did the legendary Finn, Paavo Nurmi win?

5. In what ancient Olympic event were hand weights called *halteres* used?

6. Which single person is both the Olympics' youngest and oldest gold medallist in kayaking?

7. Can you name two of the three basketball teams that defeated the United States men's team at the 2004 Olympics?

8. Which country is the only one to not win a gold medal at an Olympics they hosted?

9 Fibreglass poles were used for the first time in the pole vault and Joe Frazier won the USA's only boxing gold medal – in which Olympics?

10 Which Paralympic sport is a bowling game originating in Greece which is played by athletes with severe physical disabilities, usually sitting in wheelchairs?

11 For how many seconds can a water polo team keep possession of the ball without scoring a goal before they must hand it to the opposition?

12 Juho Saaristo is the only person to win two Olympic javelin medals at the same Games; which one?

13 In the 2008 women's basketball competition, which African nation was one of the twelve teams to qualify for the competition?

14 Which French football star lit the cauldron in the Olympic stadium with the Olympic torch at a Games hosted in Spain?

15 Only four women's athletics events have been held at every Games since 1928 – can you name two of them?

16 Which Paralympic class of track athlete is allowed to run with a sighted runner beside them as a guide: F54, T11, T56 or F13?

17 Which two Olympic sports were both invented at Springfield College in Massachusetts?

18 After losing his bout in which sport did Byun Jong-Il sit down in protest in the competition area for 67 minutes?

19 Hans-Grunner Liljenwall was the first person to: win five gold medals, be banned from the Olympics for a positive drug test or win medals in three different sports?

20 How many pigeons did Leon de Lunden shoot and kill to win a live pigeon shooting competition at the 1900 Olympics?

21 What was the name of the horse that Princess Anne rode in the three-day eventing competition at the 1976 Olympics?

22 How many gold medals did Great Britain win at the 2004 Olympics: five, nine, thirteen or eighteen?

23 Four-time gold medallist in Olympic track sprints, Fanny Blankers-Koen won her 58th and last Dutch national athletics title in 1955 – in what event?

24 Which were the first Games where officials tried to confiscate spectators' cameras as they agreed exclusive photographic rights with a single company?

25 How many cyclists completed the twelve hour cycling race held at the 1896 Olympics?

26 What food did Ecuadorian racewalker Jefferson Perez Quezada win a lifetime's free supply of after winning gold at the 1996 Olympics?

27 Which three Olympic Games gave winning athletes gold medals made of solid gold?

28 Which multiple rowing gold medallist was the British bobsleigh champion in 1989?

29 Which American won six gold medals at the 2004 Olympics?

30 What was the name of the now defunct football club which represented Great Britain at the 1900 Olympics and won the competition?

31 How old was Nadia Comaneci when she scored a perfect 10 at the 1976 Olympics?

32 In which sport did Great Britain win eight gold medals at the 2008 Olympics?

33 The Olympic flag at the 1920 Games was stolen by diving bronze medallist Haig Prieste as a prank and not returned until: 1945, 1970 or 2000?

34 Which one of the five apparatus used in rhythmic gymnastics was not used at the 2008 Olympics?

35 Can you name four of the five events in an ancient Olympics pentathlon?

36 Can you name either of the two American sprinters who made a 'black power' salute at the 1968 Olympics?

37 What is the longest swimming event for women in an Olympic pool?

38 When voting for the hosts of the 2012 Olympics got down to just two cities, what was the other city left, apart from London?

39 At the 2000 Olympics, who deprived Roger Federer of a men's singles bronze medal by beating him in a play-off match?

40 The very first event of the 1948 Olympic Games was a football qualifying match between the Netherlands and Ireland held at which English football ground?

41 Can a women's floor exercise routine in Olympic gymnastics last up to 60 seconds, up to 90 seconds, up to 120 seconds or up to 150 seconds?

42 Can you name the Swiss tennis player who became the 1992 men's singles gold medallist?

43 The International Broadcast and Press Centre at London 2012 will be as large as how many football pitches?

44 Because of the break-up of the Soviet Union, which wrestler won three Olympic gold medals, representing a different team (Soviet Union, Unified Team, Russia) each time?

45 Who became the first ever winner of the women's Olympic 3,000m steeplechase?

46 What was the shortest distance sprint raced on the track at the 1900 and 1904 Olympics?

47 Jang Mi Ran won gold in the +75kg weightlifting at the 2008 Olympics. To the nearest 10kg, can you guess how much her record clean and jerk lift was?

48 In which Canadian city were the first Winter Paralympics in 1976 held?

49 Two brothers and one sister in the same family have won almost all of the United States' taekwondo medals. What is the family's surname?

50 The Belgian road race cycling team won at the 1948 Olympics but with no officials to notice, left to go home. In what year did they receive their gold medals?

 HARD QUIZ 2

1 World War II General, George Patton, competed at the 1912 Olympics in which event?

2 Is the notch at the end of an arrow that lies against an archery bow string called the hitch, the point, the nock or the cleft?

3 How many modern Olympic Games (from 1896 onwards) featured tug of war as an Olympic sport?

4 Up until 2001, how many points did you have to score in table tennis to win a game?

5 Which one of the five apparatus used in rhythmic gymnastics will not be used at the 2012 Olympics?

6 At which Olympics was the cauldron in the Olympic stadium lit up by an archer firing a flaming arrow?

7 How many times do 3,000m steeplechasers have to leap over barriers and water jumps in a race?

8 In which Asian country was the decision announced to award the 2012 Olympics to London?

9 Which little-known tennis player from Taiwan knocked Andy Murray out of the 2008 Olympics men's singles tennis competition?

10 What is the name of the event featuring six different types of track cycling races which will first appear at an Olympics in 2012?

11 At the 1936 Olympics, which men's basketball team won silver, but scored just eight points in the final?

12 In which sport did a four-man British team including Lord Wodehouse and Teignmouth Meville win a gold medal at the 1920 Olympics?

13 Which two countries were a combined team at the 1912 Olympics, winning two golds, two silvers and three bronze medals?

14 In 1964, Japan's Osamu Watanabe won his event without giving a single point away and then retired from the sport at the age of 24. What sport was he taking part in?

15 At the Beijing 2008 Games, Ara Abrahamian threw his Olympic bronze medal away during the medal ceremony in protest and was stripped of his medal. In which sport had he won it?

16 Can you name one of the three European nations that boycotted the 1956 Olympics in protest at the Soviet Union's invasion of Hungary?

17 The father of American tennis player, Andre Agassi, competed at the 1948 and 1952 Olympics as a boxer for which country?

18 Olympic records were created in fifteen of the sixteen men's swimming events in the pool at the 2008 Olympics. Who created the other record in the 400m at Sydney in 2000?

19 Which venue has hosted its sport since 1814 but for the 2012 Olympics, is hosting a quite different sport?

20 At the 1964 Olympics, which versatile British female athlete won a gold in the long jump, a silver in the pentathlon and a bronze in the 4x100m relay?

21 In which sport did Great Britain win four gold medals, one silver and one bronze at the 2008 Games?

22 How many Olympic Games have not featured the men's hammer throw?

23 By winning the last competition held in 1924, which country is the reigning Olympic rugby champion?

24 What was Michael Phelps's best result at the 2000 Olympics?

25 In what year was it announced that London had won the right to host the 2012 Games?

26 Ricardo Blas Jr. took part in men's judo at the 2008 Olympics and became the heaviest known Olympian. Can you guess his weight to within 10kg more or less?

27 At the 1952 Olympics, which small European country knocked the Great Britain football team out of the competition, winning 5-3?

28 Which three women's football teams from Europe competed in the 2008 Olympic football competition?

29 At the 2000 Olympics, which piece of gymnastics apparatus was set 5cm too low by mistake, resulting in a number of gymnasts crashing?

30 Did American athletes win 1, 5, 17 or 21 of the 22 track and field gold medals on offer at the 1904 Olympics?

31 In what position did Zola Budd finish in the 1984 Olympics women's 3,000m final?

32 Which Olympic sport was actually invented by the founder of the modern Olympic Games, Baron Pierre de Coubertin?

33 Irini Merleni was so excited at winning gold in which combat sport in 2004 that she kissed all the judges?

34 Before London 2012, which European country had appeared at 26 Summer and Winter Olympics without winning a medal?

35 Which Paralympic sport features teams of three blind or visually-impaired players trying to score goals using a ball with bells inside?

36 At the 2004 Olympics opening ceremony, did the Greek team march out first, second, tenth or last?

37 How many boxing medals did the Great Britain team win at the 2008 Games?

38 Which famous charity owns Hadleigh Farm, the venue for the 2012 mountain biking competitions?

39 Which South American country has sent competitors to seventeen Winter or Summer Olympics without yet winning a medal?

40 At the 1908 Olympics, the three races for motor boats all saw the same number of boats finish in each race. How many?

41 Sprinter Merlene Ottey has appeared in seven Olympic Games, six times for Jamaica and once for which nation?

42 In the 1908 marathon, Charles Hefferon, the race leader, accepted a glass of champagne with two miles (3.2km) to go. In what position did he finish?

43 Which country has won more fencing medals (115 up to and including the 2008 Games) than any other nation?

44 The 1968 Paralympic Games were not held in Mexico City, but where were they held?

45 Which European country won all three croquet gold medals at the 1900 Olympics?

46 In 1956, Australian quarantine laws meant that horses for the equestrian events couldn't get to Melbourne so in which European city, a former Olympic host itself, were the equestrian events held?

47 At his peak, how many years did three-time Olympic wrestling champion, Aleksandr Karelin, go unbeaten in all competitions?

48 Who became the first men's singles tennis Olympic champion in 64 years when winning gold in 1988?

49 Is Usain Bolt's middle name: Ferdinand, St Leo, Harold or Marley?

50 What was the name of the winning horse in the horse long jump event held at the 1900 Olympics?

ANSWERS

EASY ANSWERS

Quiz 1

1. Greece
2. Karate
3. 19th century
4. Every four years
5. A bronze medal
6. 400m
7. Five
8. Football
9. China
10. Javelin

11. One oar
12. Athletics
13. Paralympics
14. The Mall
15. Cycling
16. Backstroke
17. Water polo
18. Squash
19. Rugby
20. True

21. Swimming events
22. Venus and Serena Williams
23. One event
24. Women
25. The River Thames
26. Table tennis
27. True
28. The podium
29. Five
30. Three

31. Diving
32. Barcelona
33. False

34. Swimming
35. New York
36. 1988
37. Basketball
38. Hammer throw
39. Seven
40. Usain Bolt

41. False
42. Separate events for men and women
43. Female
44. Two
45. Football
46. Eight
47. Australia
48. Weightlifting
49. Seven
50. Around 200 countries

Quiz 2

1. Four
2. Carlos Tevez (8 goals)
3. Just over 42km
4. Gymnastics
5. Badminton
6. Women
7. Synchronised swimming
8. Eleven
9. True
10. Cycling

11. Ten
12. Lightning Bolt
13. True
14. Argentina
15. Diving

16. The marathon
17. Brussels
18. Paralympic events
19. Cycling
20. London

21. Athens
22. Tennis
23. Male gymnasts
24. 1896
25. Yes
26. Boxing
27. Sailing
28. North
29. Beijing 2008
30. Two oars

31. Olympia
32. Male gymnasts

33. 2012 Olympics
34. Brazil (17)
35. Triathlon
36. Breaststroke, backstroke (back crawl) and butterfly
37. Atlanta
38. Pierre
39. Taekwondo
40. Cycling

41. 1948
42. Heptathlon
43. Eight
44. Vancouver
45. At an Olympic swimming pool
46. Fencing
47. 1996
48. False (1900 and 1904)
49. Tennis
50. Sir Chris Hoy

 MEDIUM ANSWERS

Quiz 1

1. 776 BCE
2. Athens
3. Rowing
4. Brands Hatch
5. Tirunesh Dibaba
6. 190m long
7. 4 metres
8. London
9. A running race
10. Cape Town

11. French
12. Five
13. Donovan Bailey

14. Four
15. 1984
16. Africa
17. Velodrome
18. Danny Boyle
19. Latin
20. One

21. Lighter
22. 17,000
23. 1928
24. Switzerland
25. Three
26. A bear
27. Matthew Pinsent
28. Four

29. Rugby Sevens
30. 2000

31. 400,000 meals per day
32. Iraq
33. Triple jump
34. 200m
35. A medical doctor
36. Taekwondo
37. Their boat!
38. Citius, Altius, Fortius
39. Super Heavyweight
40. 1,500m

41. Baseball
42. The vault
43. Decathlon
44. A sergeant in the British Army
45. It was made of wood
46. Discus
47. The 110m / 100m hurdles
48. Canada
49. Cameroon
50. Chris Hoy

Quiz 2

1. Munich
2. Hard-boiled eggs
3. Four
4. Carl Lewis
5. Fencing
6. Breaststroke
7. Three gold
8. Lawn bowls
9. Piccadilly Line
10. 90m

11. 1952
12. Birmingham
13. 1924 Olympics

14. Fencing
15. 1960 Olympics
16. Archery
17. Rhythmic gymnastics
18. 1988 Olympics
19. Women's hammer throw
20. 19 years old

21. Oldest (38 years old)
22. 1908
23. 1928 Amsterdam
24. Venus Williams
25. 10km open water
26. Beach volleyball
27. Eight
28. Wrestling
29. Brazil
30. Sir Clive Woodward

31. 1936
32. Eleanor Simmonds
33. True
34. *Chariots of Fire*
35. 800m
36. The baton
37. Stockholm, 1912
38. Visually impaired athletes
39. Five
40. Ian Thorpe

41. Eleven
42. Argentina
43. None
44 Two
45. Once
46. Greenwich Park
47. Middleweight
48. The javelin (current Olympic record: 90.57m)
49. Right
50. Roger Federer

Quiz 3

1. True
2. The Orbit
3. 8.34m
4. Four
5. Athletics
6. Rhythmic gymnastics
7. 50 metres
8. District (60 stations)
9. Seven-a-side
10. Trampolining

11. Hungary
12. The five rings
13. Three
14. 1968
15. 1928
16. Koka
17. Afghanistan
18. St Louis
19. 15m high
20. Nadia Comaneci

21. Johnny Weissmuller
22. Nastia Liukin
23. Carlos Tevez
24. One
25. Swimming
26. Argentina
27. 5.05m
28. Finn
29. Shooting
30. 100 years (1996)

31. Javelin, shot put, discus
32. Sailing
33. Archery
34. 50km
35. Cycling
36. Silver
37. Football

38. Eleven
39. Silver
40. Princess Anne

41. 7.26kg
42. The 1996 Atlanta Olympics
43. Six
44. The United States
45. 1908
46. Bermuda
47. One minute
48. Uneven bars
49. Brazil
50. Steffi Graf

Quiz 4

1. Front crawl
2. Cuba
3. Helsinki
4. Fencing
5. 10,000m
6. Bob Beamon
7. One
8. George Foreman
9. Honduras
10. Argentina

11. 1988 Olympics
12. 3,000m steeplechase
13. Two (Greco-Roman and Freestyle)
14. True
15. The Water Polo Arena
16. Middlesex
17. Ippon
18. 400m hurdles
19. Jason Kenny
20. 400m

21. The London Eye
22. Zimbabwe

23. 21 points
24. Taekwondo
25. Field hockey
26. Ten
27. Jurgen Hingsen
28. Rowing
29. China, Singapore, Germany, South Korea
30. Spain

31. 1900
32. Audley Harrison
33. Synchronised swimming
34. 1908
35. 2,000m
36. Women's discus
37. Zeus
38. Switzerland
39. Taekwondo
40. 19

41. Norway
42. 15m
43. India
44. Cuba
45. 22
46. Nicolas Massau
47. Australia
48. Athens 2004
49. China
50. Three

Quiz 5

1. China
2. Pommel horse
3. False
4. Javelin
5. A beaver
6. Heavyweight
7. Hockey
8. 70 years old

9. Basketball
10. 1,500m, 4x400m relay, 110m hurdles

11. Dorset
12. Cycling
13. 5,000m
14. Five
15. Carl Lewis
16. Archery
17. 60 minutes
18. 55 triathletes
19. London 1908
20. Basketball court

21. 16 years of age
22. Hockey
23. 1968 Olympics
24. Germany
25. Linford Christie
26. Twelve
27. Boxing
28. Nigeria
29. One
30. Dressage

31. 32 minutes
32. A motorboat
33. Sydney 2000
34. A long distance race
35. Gymnastics
36. High jump
37. *E.T. the Extra-Terrestrial*
38. Sailing
39. Fourteen
40. Great Britain

41. Emperor Theodosius I
42. True
43. Silver
44. Weightlifting
45. Eight

46. Had one leg amputated
47. London
48. 1956 Melbourne
49. 78,000km
50. The discus

Quiz 6

1. Spain
2. His boxing gloves
3. Japan
4. Louis Smith
5. Michael Phelps
6. Rope climbing, parallel bars, long horse gymnastics
7. Russia
8. Higher
9. Serbia
10. 800m

11. 1908 Olympics
12. Seventh
13. South Korea
14. Oddjob
15. Weightlifting
16. 40km
17. The Ukraine
18. Sixteen years old
19. 1984
20. A dog

21. 1996
22. Visually impaired
23. Paris, 1900
24. Daley Thompson
25. 2kg
26. Great Britain
27. True
28. Hungary
29. Steven Hooker
30. Chest

31. Mountain biking
32. Five
33. 1992
34. Wheelchair basketball
35. 2004
36. Over 18m
37. Land's End
38. Sarah Stevenson
39. Two minutes
40. Larisa Latynina

41. Over six hours
42. Sydney 2000
43. True
44. Yes
45. Discus, hammer throw
46. Mountain biking
47. Spain
48. The piste
49. Over 11,000
50. Paris 1900

Quiz 7

1. True
2. Deuce
3. Mintonette
4. Outside lane
5. Three
6. True
7. Ten
8. Jacques Rogge
9. Germaine Mason
10. Backstroke

11. Women's pole vault
12. Beth Tweddle
13. Belgium
14. Handball
15. Argentina
16. 110m hurdles
17. South Korea

18. Wembley Arena
19. Japan
20. Anchor

21. Fencing
22. 1984 Olympics
23. Three
24. 1936
25. 2008
26. Greenwich Park
27. Three (discus, hammer, shot put)
28. Four
29. Four minutes
30. Marathon

31. Seven
32. Floor exercise and the vault
33. Bradley Wiggins
34. Canada
35. Two rounds
36. Synchronised swimming
37. Peru
38. The discus
39. Cuba
40. Stockholm 1912

41. Hammer throw
42. Seoul 1988
43. 1900
44. New South Wales
45. Hyde Park
46. Keirin
47. Archery
48. Three metres
49. 43 seconds
50. 100m, 200m, 4x100m relay, long jump

Quiz 8

1. Archery

2. Shot put
3. Both ends
4. Blue
5. Football
6. USA, China, Russia
7. 400m
8. 800m, 1,500m
9. Manchester
10. The Olympic Stadium

11. True
12. Yelena Isinbayeva
13. 60 shots
14. Twelve years old
15. Rome
16. Sydney 2000
17. Melbourne, 1956
18. 200m
19. 400m hurdles
20. Ray Ewry

21. 1924
22. Kayaking
23. Eight
24. 20 points
25. 1968
26. Sydney 2000
27. Three
28. Fencing
29. The United States
30. Judo

31. They are disqualified
32. Three
33. Norway
34. Berlin
35. Four
36. None
37. The Basketball Arena
38. Asia
39. Denmark
40. Eventing

41. Wrestling
42. Javelin
43. Badminton
44. Windsurfing
45. Shawn Johnson
46. Fencing
47. A free transport ticket
48. Turkey, Hungary, Bulgaria, Austria
49. The Madison
50. Three

Quiz 9

1. True
2. Three
3. False
4. Seven
5. 1936
6. Women's 100m hurdles
7. The Serpentine
8. 1980
9. True
10. Three

11. Pistol shooting
12. Justin Gatlin
13. Freestyle
14. A medical surgeon
15. Mongolia, China, the Dominican Republic
16. 1964
17. Putney Bridge
18. 1988
19. Six
20. Turkey

21. Wembley Stadium
22. China, Japan, North Korea
23. Moscow
24. John Williams
25. 1996 Atlanta

26. Brazil and Germany
27. Russia
28. 20km
29. Flyweight
30. Equestrianism

31. Shooting
32. 1936
33. Great Britain
34. Seventeen
35. Tunisia
36. A shot (shot put)
37. Namibia
38. Argentina
39. 400m hurdles
40. 1936

41. Japan
42. Bulgaria
43. 1984
44. Africa
45. 2.18m
46. Gears and brakes
47. India
48. Essex
49. Handball
50. Peru

Quiz 10

1. Rowing
2. Three
3. 21 points
4. Forgetting his lifejacket
5. Hampden Park
6. Boxing
7. 200m, 80m hurdles
8. 25
9. Every hour
10. Table tennis

11. Albania

12. Keirin, sprint, team sprint
13. Heavyweight
14. The 400m Individual Medley
15. 10 points
16. Tia Hellebaut
17. 20%
18. Twice
19. Madrid, Moscow
20. 130km

21. High jump
22. 2004
23. Finland
24. Croquet
25. Five
26. At the 2000 Games
27. Usain Bolt (100m, 200m, 4x100m relay)
28. Eight
29. Standing, kneeling, prone (lying down)
30. Sweden

31. Triple jump
32. Fifteen years old
33. 1948
34. Three
35. Weightlifting, wrestling, taekwondo
36. 1896 Olympics
37. 11 hours 40 minutes
38. Muhammad Ali
39. 2004
40. As long as both men were still standing

41. Amsterdam
42. DDR (East Germany)
43. 6-6 (six games all)
44. Nine
45. Los Angeles
46. Faster

47. An amputee
48. Rome
49. False
50. United States

Quiz 11

1. 10km (10,000m)
2. Kneel
3. Montreal
4. A combined shooting competition and 3,000m cross-country run
5. A duck-billed platypus
6. Six
7. The Maracana
8. One
9. Wenlock
10. The 5,000m

11. New York
12. Australia
13. Lausanne
14. Luz Long
15. The hoop
16. Cuba
17. Antwerp
18. Eleven million
19. Boris Johnson
20. Seven times

21. Eleven years old
22. Nine
23. Table tennis
24. Pole vault
25. Isle of Wight
26. Triathlon
27. 80,000 spectators
28. Kelly Holmes
29. Munich
30. Kenya

31. Rowing
32. Evander Holyfield
33. Beijing 2008
34. Korea
35. India
36. Three
37. Cycling
38. True (45% is underground)
39. In bare feet
40. Four

41. Long jump, triple jump
42. Nadia Comaneci
43. Cyprus
44. Five
45. Olga Korbut
46. Shot put, long jump, high jump, javelin
47. 1996 Atlanta
48. Two seconds
49. Russia
50. Brazil

Quiz 12

1. Melbourne 1956
2. Nine (eight rowers plus the cox)
3. Freestyle
4. Lightweight
5. BMX racing
6. Water polo
7. The Olympic flame
8. Goose
9. Foil
10. Over 7,000

11. Yelena Isinbayeva
12. Sunday
13. 100m, 200m, 4x100m relay, 80m hurdles

14. Kevin Garnett
15. Shaved her head
16. Cuba
17. 70m
18. Larisa Latynina
19. Table tennis
20. The 1996 Olympics

21. Under 36 seconds
22. Five
23. Indoor volleyball
24. Barcelona
25. Cycling
26. 1904 Olympics
27. Danny Boyle
28. Kookaburra
29. Diving
30. Greenwich Park

31. 3,000m women's steeplechase
32. Golf
33. One
34. St Louis and London
35. Carli Lloyd
36. Trampolining
37. Hungary, Soviet Union (USSR)
38. Seven
39. Light-heavyweight
40. Tug of war

41. Yugoslavia
42. Heidelberg
43. Chicago Bulls
44. Fencing
45. 4,000m
46. Baseball
47. Seven seconds
48. 1,500m
49. Gymnastics
50. USA

Quiz 13

1. Red, green, yellow, blue and black
2. 1904
3. Rowing
4. The 3,000m Steeplechase
5. Wrestling
6. True
7. Heavier
8. 1992
9. 2008
10. The opening ceremony

11. 10,000m
12. St James' Park (Newcastle United), Old Trafford (Manchester United)
13. Boxing, baseball
14. Ten
15. None
16. Munich 1972
17. 4x100m running
18. Tennis mixed doubles
19. Paris (1900 and 1924)
20. Dawn Fraser

21. Sailing
22. A crown of olive leaves given to winners
23. Three (1984, 1988 and 1992)
24. Cuba
25. Épée
26. The Fosbury Flop
27. Judo
28. The United States
29. 1960
30. Shot put

31. René Lacoste
32. 8,000
33. Heavyweight

34. Discus and shot put
35. Mountain biking
36. Four
37. Newham, Hackney, Waltham Forest, Tower Hamlets, Greenwich
38. 2.5 metres
39. Boxing
40. Over 100kg

41. New York City
42. Latvia
43. Yelena Isinbayeva
44. Hockey
45. 2008 Beijing
46. Jesse Owens
47. Rhythmic gymnastics
48. A pair of underpants (Y-fronts to be precise!)
49. USA
50. Pommel horse

Quiz 14

1. Los Angeles 1984
2. Five
3. Butterfly
4. Wimbledon
5. Silver medal
6. 10 km
7. Golf
8. Three
9. 1908
10. Moscow

11. Athens
12. Zola Budd
13. Decathlon
14. Great Barrier Reef
15. Barcelona 1992
16. Under 127 minutes
17. Trampolining

18. Paul Hamm
19. Sydney
20. Windsurfing

21. South Korea
22. 100m freestyle
23. Nine
24. South Africa
25. *Slumdog Millionaire, 28 Days Later*
26. Pentathlon
27. South Korea
28. Moscow, New York City, Madrid, Paris
29. Horseguards Parade
30. Four

31. Seventh
32. Equestrianism
33. 43 points
34. Wheelchair tennis
35. 1,000kg
36. Discus
37. 1984
38. False (Silver medals in 1896)
39. Shooting
40. Brazil

41. Flyweight
42. Tuberculosis
43. Stockholm
44. Steve Backley
45. Visually impaired
46. Baron Pierre de Coubertin
47. Hampton Court Palace
48. Silver medals
49. Waterford Crystal
50. Athena, Phevos

Quiz 15

1. China

2. High jump
3. 10m
4. USA
5. France
6. 1940
7. Four more players (eleven per side)
8. 226 medals behind
9. 1996, 2000, 2004 and 2008
10. Ken Livingstone

11. Lithuania
12. Modern pentathlon
13. Hampden Park, Glasgow
14. The Czech Republic
15. 1924
16. Canada
17. One
18. Men's marathon
19. Third
20. Men wearing 25kg of armour

21. Shooting
22. Weightlifting, athletics, gymnastics
23. The women's 100m sprint (athletics)
24. Four
25. An Australian teenager, Ian Wing
26. White City Stadium
27. The pentathlon
28. Just over £5
29. Millennium Stadium, Cardiff
30. 1956 Melbourne

31. Matthew Pinsent
32. Stockholm
33. Archery
34. San Juan, Saint Petersburg, Seville, Stockholm
35. Ten

36. Ireland
37. 47
38. China
39. Five
40. Silver

41. Tirunesh Dibaba
42. True

43. Four (two gold, two silver)
44. Mandeville
45. True
46. Denmark
47. Gymnastics
48. 5,000 spectators
49. A stopwatch
50. His heart

WINTER OLYMPICS ANSWERS

Quiz 1

1. 2006
2. True
3. The 2010 Winter Olympics
4. Curling
5. Biathlon
6. Italy
7. Silver
8. Head first
9. A snowman
10. Ice hockey

11. Ten
12. St Moritz
13. More than a dozen
14. Mogul
15. Canada
16. Russia
17. Chemmy Alcott
18. Eight
19. Speed skating
20. Luge

21. Soviet Union
22. Canada
23. Austrian
24. Women's figure skating
25. 10,000m

26. 1984
27. 1992 and 1994
28. Canada
29. Four
30. Skeleton

31. Boxing
32. Great Britain
33. Norwegian
34. Germany and Japan
35. Three
36. London 1908
37. Squaw Valley
38. Tonya Harding
39. 1976
40. Lindsey Jacobellis

41. Franklin D Roosevelt
42. Four (1948, 2002, 2006, 2010)
43. Twelve
44. One
45. Speed skating
46. Germany
47. South Korea, Austria
48. Australia
49. Entered the bobsleigh facing backwards
50. Snowboarding parallel slalom

Quiz 2

1. Curling
2. Slovakia
3. Twice (both in Japan)
4. 82
5. Speed skating
6. Eight
7. Peru, Pakistan
8. Owls
9. Ice hockey
10. Gold

11. Two woman bobsleigh
12. South Korea
13. 11
14. Alain Baxter
15. 7.5km
16. Norway
17. Figure skating
18. Speed skating
19. Finland
20. Twelve

21. Snowboard cross
22. Soviet Union
23. The 1936 Olympics
24. Japan

25. Skeleton
26. Turin
27. USA and Switzerland
28. 1980 Lake Placid
29. Russia, France, Germany
30. One

31. Flying Tomato
32. Four
33. Biathlon
34. Skiing
35. Four
36. Yugoslavia, Soviet Union
37. Colombia, Cayman Islands
38. 19.1kg
39. *Cool Runnings*
40. Ice hockey

41. Ski jumping
42. Austria
43. Ice hockey
44. Bode Miller
45. 50 years
46. Chamonix
47. *Bolero*
48. Denver
49. 10,000m
50. 282m (his first jump was 144m, his second, 138m)

 HARD ANSWERS

Quiz 1

1. Lasse Viren
2. Richard Thompson
3. Equestrianism
4. Nine
5. Long jump

6. Birgit Fischer
7. Argentina, Puerto Rico, Lithuania
8. Canada (Montreal 1976)
9. 1964 Tokyo
10. Boccia

HARD ANSWERS

11. Thirty seconds
12. 1912 Stockholm Games (single-handed and two-handed javelin events)
13. Mali
14. Michel Platini
15. Discus, 4x100m relay, high jump, 100m sprint
16. T11
17. Basketball and volleyball
18. Boxing
19. Banned from the Olympics for a positive drug test
20. 21

21. Goodwill
22. Nine
23. Shot put
24. Amsterdam, 1928
25. Two
26. Yoghurt
27. 1904, 1908 and 1912
28. Steve Redgrave
29. Michael Phelps
30. Upton Park FC

31. Fourteen
32. Cycling
33. 2000
34. The ball
35. The discus, javelin, jumping, running, wrestling
36. Tommie Smith, John Carlos
37. 800m
38. Paris
39. Arnaud Di Pasquale
40. Fratton Park

41. Up to 90 seconds
42. Marc Rosset
43. Six
44. Aleksandr Karelin

45. Gulnara Galkina-Samitova
46. 60m
47. 186kg
48. Toronto
49. Lopez
50. 2010

Quiz 2

1. Modern pentathlon
2. The nock
3. Five
4. 21
5. The rope
6. Barcelona 1992
7. 35 (7 water jumps and 28 barriers)
8. Singapore
9. Lu Yen-Hsun
10. The Omnium

11. Canada
12. Polo
13. Australia and New Zealand
14. Freestyle wrestling
15. Greco-Roman wrestling
16. Switzerland, Spain, the Netherlands
17. Iran
18. Ian Thorpe
19. Lord's cricket ground
20. Mary Rand

21. Sailing
22. One
23. The United States
24. Fifth in the 200m butterfly
25. 2005
26. 210kg
27. Luxembourg
28. Germany, Norway, Sweden
29. The vaulting table
30. 21 out of 22

31. Seventh
32. Modern pentathlon
33. Wrestling
34. Monaco
35. Goalball
36. Last
37. Three
38. The Salvation Army
39. Bolivia
40. One

41. Slovenia
42. Second
43. France
44. Tel Aviv
45. France
46. Stockholm
47. Thirteen years
48. Miloslav Mečíř
49. St Leo
50. Extra-Dry